PROTECTING OUR COMMON, SACRED HOME

PROTECTING OUR COMMON, SACRED HOME

POPE FRANCIS

and

PROCESS THOUGHT

DAVID RAY GRIFFIN

PROCESS
CENTURY
PRESS

ANOKA, MINNESOTA 2016

Protecting our Common, Sacred Home: Pope Francis and Process Thought

© 2016 Process Century Press

Process Century Press
RiverHouse LLC
802 River Lane
Anoka, MN 55303

Process Century Press books are published in association with the International Process Network.

Cover: Susanna Mennicke

VOLUME XII: TOWARD ECOLOGICAL CIVILIZATION SERIES
JEANYNE B. SLETTOM, GENERAL EDITOR

ISBN 978-1-940447-24-7
Printed in the United States of America

CONTENTS

We live in the ending of an age. But the ending of the modern period differs from the ending of previous periods, such as the classical or the medieval. The amazing achievements of modernity make it possible, even likely, that its end will also be the end of civilization, of many species, or even of the human species. At the same time, we are living in an age of new beginnings that give promise of an ecological civilization. Its emergence is marked by a growing sense of urgency and deepening awareness that the changes must go to the roots of what has led to the current threat of catastrophe.

In June 2015, the 10th Whitehead International Conference was held in Claremont, CA. Called "Seizing an Alternative: Toward an Ecological Civilization," it claimed an organic, relational, integrated, nondual, and processive conceptuality is needed, and that Alfred North Whitehead provides this in a remarkably comprehensive and rigorous way. We proposed that he could be "the philosopher of ecological civilization." With the help of those who have come to an ecological vision in other ways, the conference explored this Whiteheadian alternative, showing how it can provide the shared vision so urgently needed.

The judgment underlying this effort is that contemporary research and scholarship is still enthralled by the 17th century view of nature articulated by Descartes and reinforced by Kant. Without freeing our minds of this objectifying and reductive understanding of the world, we are not likely to direct our actions wisely in response to the crisis to which this tradition has led us. Given the ambitious goal of replacing now dominant patterns of thought with one that would redirect us toward ecological civilization, clearly more is needed than a single conference. Fortunately, a larger platform is developing that includes the conference and looks beyond it. It is named Pando Populus (pandopopulous.com) in honor of the world's largest and oldest organism, an aspen grove.

As a continuation of the conference, and in support of the larger initiative of Pando Populus, we are publishing this series, appropriately named "Toward Ecological Civilization."

~John B. Cobb, Jr.

OTHER BOOKS IN THIS SERIES

INTRODUCTION

IN THE PRESENT CENTURY, the world has become more concerned about what climate scientists are saying about the dangers
of global warming and its resulting climate changes. Many scientists
have warned, in fact, that if the global warming continues, it will
eventually bring civilization to an end—perhaps within the century.[1]

In spite of these warnings, however, the political world, especially
in the United States, has failed to respond vigorously. Part of this failure can be explained by the typical concern of politicians to focus on
immediate problems, leaving future generations to worry about what
seem to be longer-term problems (in spite of the fact that climate
change has already become serious in many places). But a significant
portion of the failure is attributable, especially in the United States, to
the success of an effort, funded massively by fossil-fuel corporations,
to convince people that global warming is not real, or at least not
caused by the burning of fossil fuels.[2]

By early 2015, the hope for saving civilization seemed to rest
on the big United Nations meeting (COP21) in Paris at the end of
that year. The hope was that the various nations would pledge to
reduce their own use of fossil fuels sufficiently to prevent catastrophic

1

climate change. The generally accepted view was that this goal could be achieved if the increase in the planet's average temperature since pre-industrial times remains below 2°C (3.6°F).

Unfortunately, given that at the time of the conference the increase of 0.8°C (1.4°F) was already producing terrible consequences, leading climate scientists said that the increase in the global temperature must be kept to 1°C or, if that proves impossible, no more than 1.5°C. The target of 2°C, said top climate scientist James Hansen, is a "recipe for disaster."[3] By October, reported Hansen, the global temperature for the preceding 12 months was 1.25°C above pre-industrial times, leaving little room in the 1.5°C budget.[4]

But in June 2015, there occurred a powerful intervention into the discussion by Pope Francis. His encyclical, *Laudato Si'* [Praise Be to You], subtitled *On Care for Our Common Home*, called for swift action on climate change.[5]

Almost simultaneously with the official publication of this encyclical, there was the biggest-ever conference of the movement known as process thought, based primarily on the philosophy of Alfred North Whitehead.[6] This conference discussed various ways in which process thought could be helpful with respect to the global environmental crisis, especially climate change.

The conference was organized by the world's leading process philosopher and theologian, John B. Cobb, Jr., who had been dealing with the ecological crisis for many decades, having in 1971 published the first book on environmental ethics, *Is It Too Late? A Theology of Ecology* (1972). Cobb later co-authored a major book, entitled *For the Common Good: Redirecting the Economy Toward Community, the Environment, and a Sustainable Future* (1989), with the founder of ecological economics, Herman Daly.[7] After writing many more books on these topics, Cobb at age 90 was still going strong.

The conference, called "Seizing an Alternative," was written against the slogan, "There is no alternative" (TINA), which was inspired by former British Prime Minister Margaret Thatcher. The slogan means that, for modern societies to develop, there is no alternative to economic liberalism—with its focus on free markets, free trade, and capitalist globalization. Cobb's conference was organized to show that process thought, with its distinctive views on social thought, especially economics, as well as philosophy and religion, does provide an alternative.

After that conference was finished, Cobb immediately organized the writing of a book entitled *For Our Common Home: Process-Relational Responses to Laudato Si'*. In the preface, in which Cobb explained the purpose that led him (along with his co-editor, Ignacio Castuera, and the other contributors) to write this book, he said: "We resolved to merge our little movement into the great one that we hope Pope Francis will lead."[8]

The purpose of the present book is to show why process thought—meaning process philosophy, theology, and social/economic thought—provides a natural and helpful context in which to expound and defend the ecological message in the pope's 2015 encyclical.

Given the fact that Cobb and I are both liberal Protestants, it is not surprising that we differ with the pope's position on a number of issues.[9] What *is* surprising—indeed, it seems almost miraculous, given the history of the papacy since the death of Pope John XXIII in 1963—is that we now have a pope who, besides being beloved around the world, has issued an encyclical with which we so thoroughly agree.

One remarkable thing about the encyclical is that Pope Francis addressed not simply fellow Catholics, or even fellow Christians in general. Rather, he said: "I wish to address every person living on this planet" (LS 3 [meaning *Laudato Si'*, paragraph 3]). In speaking of the "Earth as Home," observed George Lakoff, the pope "triggers a frame in which all the people of the world are a family, living in a common home."[10]

Also remarkable is how seriously Pope Francis takes the environmental crisis, saying "we need only take a frank look at the facts to see that our common home is falling into serious disrepair" (LS 61).

Indeed, saying that "the post-industrial period may well be remembered as one of the most irresponsible in history" (LS 165), he indicates that this period has been, in fact, the *most* irresponsible: "Never have we so hurt and mistreated our common home as we have in the last two hundred years" (LS 53). In speaking of "we" here, the pope is referring primarily to modern Western civilization.

In an address to the United Nations, Pope Francis probably made his strongest statement about the seriousness of the situation, saying: "The ecological crisis, and the large-scale destruction of biodiversity, can threaten the very existence of the human species."[11]

The first part of this book focuses on "Why We Have Been Led to Destroy Our Home." The second part is devoted to "Reconstruction to Save Our Sacred Home." Rather than being primarily a commentary on the pope's encyclical, this book discusses it from the perspective of process thought, showing how this perspective, besides reinforcing the pope's stance, can also explain why this stance need not be undermined by traditional theological difficulties, such as the problem of evil.

NOTES

1   See David Ray Griffin, *Unprecedented: Can Civilization Survive the Ecological Crisis?* (Atlanta: Clarity Press, 2015), Introduction.

2   Ibid., Chapter 11, "Climate Change Denial."

3   David Spratt, "NASA Climate Chief: Labor's Targets a 'Recipe for Disaster,'" Climate Code Red, 27 January 2011.

4   James Hansen, et al, "Young People's Burden: Requirement of Negative CO_2 Emissions," Earth System Dynamics 4 October 2016 (in peer review).

5   "Encyclical Letter Laudato Si' of the Holy Father Francis on Care for Our Common Home." vatican

6   Although Whitehead himself called his position the "philosophy of organism," it came to be known as "process philosophy," because Whitehead's major work was named *Process and Reality*.

7 Herman E. Daly and John B. Cobb, Jr., *For the Common Good: Redirecting the Economy toward Community, the Environment, and a Sustainable Future* (1989), updated and expanded ed. (Boston: Beacon Press, 1994).

8 John B. Cobb and Ignacio Castuera, eds., *For Our Common Home: Process-Relational Responses to Laudato Si'* (Anoka, MN: Process Century Press, 2015), v.

9 The worst feature of the pope's encyclical, from our perspective, is his dismissal of the view that one of the most important ways in which our common home could be protected would be to stop further population growth (LA 50). This is one of the few cases in which Catholic social teaching is an impediment, rather than an aid, to the development of a helpful position on the ecological crisis.

10 George Lakoff, "Pope Francis Gets the Moral Framing Right," Reader Supported News, 27 June 2015.

11 Ryan Teague Beckwith, "Transcript: Read the Speech Pope Francis Gave to the United Nations," *Time,* 25 September 2015.

PART ONE

Why We Have Been
Led To Destroy
Our Common Home

CHAPTER ONE

False God

ONE OF THE REASONS that modern Western civilization has been destroying its home is that, insofar as it has affirmed the existence of a divine creator, it has held a false view of God. This false view involves both (i) the nature of the world that God has created and (ii) the power of God.

GOD AS CREATOR

POPE FRANCIS ON NATURE

When Cardinal Jorge Mario Bergoglio of Buenos Aires was selected to be the next pope, he chose to be named after St. Francis of Assisi, "the man of poverty, the man of peace, the man who loves and protects creation" — the same created world "with which we don't have such a good relationship."[1] In choosing this name, the new pope was taking the name of the saint who "addressed creatures as 'sisters' and 'brothers,' that is, as equals, not as subjects to be dominated."[2]

The pope's acceptance of St. Francis's attitude is reflected in his criticism of modernity's "excessive anthropocentrism," which leads to a technocracy that "sees nature as an insensate order," as "an object of utility, as raw material to be hammered into useful shape" (LS 115). By contrast, the pope says, all creatures "have an intrinsic value independent of their usefulness. Each organism, as a creature of God, is good and admirable in itself" (LS 140).

In line with this rejection of anthropomorphism, the encyclical of Pope Francis says:

> [W]e must forcefully reject the notion that our being created in God's image and given dominion over the earth justifies absolute domination over other creatures.... Clearly, the Bible has no place for a tyrannical anthropocentrism unconcerned for other creatures. (LS 67, 68)

PROCESS THOUGHT ON NATURE

The pope's view here rejects the traditional attitude of modern Western Christianity, according to which, in John Cobb's words, the nonhuman world does not have "any value in itself. Its value lies entirely in its usefulness to people," who alone "have intrinsic worth."[3]

In articulating an alternative to this anthropocentric view, Cobb wrote:

> Whitehead's philosophy pictures for us a world filled with real events, each having its own intrinsic value. Especially those that are alive significantly share with us in feeling and activity. It is therein that the needed attitude of love, concern, or reverence for living things is adequately and rationally grounded.

This philosophy, Cobb added, "describes these real and valuable events as interrelated and interconnected in just the way that is implied by the ecological attitude."[4]

The older view, according to which only human beings have intrinsic value, was rooted primarily in the philosophy of René Descartes, who articulated an absolute dualism between the human mind (or soul) and the rest of the world, described as composed entirely of insensate matter.

This dualism was very helpful to the drive of modernity to subject the entire world to technological manipulation for human comfort and profit. For example, it aided the desire of medical science to engage in vivisection. To overcome people's qualms about inflicting pain on dogs, Descartes explained that their yelps did not mean that they felt pain: the yelps were purely mechanical reactions.[5]

More generally, the dualistic worldview, according to which nature has no value except its value for human purposes, has been used to justify a completely exploitative view of the world, which has led to the ecological crisis.

POPE FRANCIS AND PROCESS THOUGHT AGREE

In spite of its helpfulness for exploiting the natural world, Descartes' dualism was manifestly inadequate for describing reality. In addition to the fact that few if any people can really think of their dogs and cats as mere machines, with no feelings, it has proven impossible to defend, either philosophically or scientifically, any line below which there is no experience. Put positively, the pope's view of the world, according to which all creatures have intrinsic value, is now supported by both science and philosophy—with microbiologists, for example, showing that even bacteria have experience.[6]

Accordingly, the hitherto dominant position of Christian philosophy and theology, according to which God created a machine-like world, implies a false view of God. The idea of God as having created a cosmic machine, in which nothing has intrinsic value except human minds (and perhaps angels), gives us one view of the universe's creator. A universe in which all creatures have intrinsic value implies a very different view of our creator—a creator who enters into loving relations with all creatures, rather than controlling them externally.

THE POWER OF GOD

Pope Francis also appears to hold a view of divine power that is more similar to that of process theology than to that of traditional theism.

THE TRADITIONAL DOCTRINE OF DIVINE POWER

The picture of God as the creator of a world-machine fit with the traditional doctrine of omnipotence, according to which God can completely control all events in the world.

- St. Augustine said that God "is called Almighty for no other reason than he can do whatsoever he willeth and his omnipotent will is not impeded by the will of any creature." As a result, Augustine added, "the will of the Omnipotent is always undefeated."[7]

- God is called omnipotent, John Calvin said, because "he regulates all things according to his secret plan, which depends solely upon itself." Human beings "can accomplish nothing," Calvin added, "except by God's secret command."[8]

- According to Martin Luther, "nothing happens but at [God's] will," so that "there can be no 'free-will' in man, or angel, or in any creature."[9] Although some theologians have argued that God determined our actions only in relation to ultimate salvation, so that we are free in relation to daily matters such as how to spend our money, "that very free-will," insisted Luther, "is overruled by the free-will of God."[10]

OMNIPOTENCE VS. CLIMATE SCIENCE

This idea of God, which has continued to be held in conservative Christian circles, has led many conservative Christians to deny climate science—which says that the burning of fossil fuels has caused global warming, which in turn has resulted in climate change. In other Christian circles, a modified version of divine omnipotence is held, according to which God allows for human freedom in most instances. According to this version, however, God fully determines the actions of the nonhuman world, while having the power to determine even human behavior whenever God wishes.

In both versions of divine omnipotence, therefore, nothing occurs in the world that God really does not want to happen. So human civilization could be destroyed by global warming only if God freely allows it. If God does not want human civilization to be destroyed, then human actions could not cause this destruction, so there is no reason to fear anthropogenic global warming. This attitude is widespread, even in the U.S. Congress.

For example, Republican Senator James Inhofe of Oklahoma has written a book called *The Greatest Hoax*, in which he argues that our future is threatened not by global warming, but only by—as the subtitle of his book says—*The Global Warming Conspiracy*. Citing a passage from the first book of the Bible, Inhofe said: "This is what a lot of alarmists forget. God is still up there, and He promised to maintain the seasons." Accordingly, it is arrogant, said Inhofe, to "think that we, human beings, would be able to change what He is doing in the climate."[11]

When Republicans regained control of the Senate in 2015, Inhofe was made the chairman of the Senate Committee on Environment and Public Works—a position that he had previously held from 2003 to 2007. With Inhofe as chairman, there was no chance that the Senate would pass legislation to curb the use of fossil fuels.

The same view of divine omnipotence has also been held by members of the House of Representatives. For example, Republican Congressman John Shimkus of Illinois used the same biblical verse as Inhofe. Calling it "the infallible word of God," Shimkus said, "That's the way it's going to be for his creation.... The Earth will end only when God declares it's time to be over."[12]

Likewise, talk-show host Rush Limbaugh took issue with Secretary of State John Kerry's statement that climate change is "a challenge to our responsibilities as the guardians... of God's creation." Limbaugh replied: "If you believe in God, then intellectually you cannot believe in manmade global warming." We should not worry about human-caused global warming, Limbaugh added, because we are not "[so] omnipotent that we can...destroy the climate."[13]

This belief in divine omnipotence is also held by many other Christians. For example, Calvin Beisner, whose organization put out an "Evangelical Declaration on Global Warming,"[14] said that to believe that global warming could lead to catastrophe would be "an insult to God."[15]

OMNIPOTENCE BELIEF AND U.S. CLIMATE COMPLACENCY

Insofar as people accept this view of divine power, it would tend, one would assume, to promote complacency about climate change. The evidence suggests that this is indeed the case.

On the one hand, a poll in 2013 indicated that, as the headline of a *Washington Post* article put it, "Americans Are Less Worried about Climate Change than Almost Anyone Else." That is, people in the United States take threats from climate change less seriously than do people in any of the other industrialized countries.[16]

In 2014, a poll involving 20 major countries showed that, as one story put it, the United States "leads the world in climate denial." When asked whether climate change is "a natural phenomenon that happens from time to time" (rather than being caused by human activity), 52% of Americans said Yes, compared with only 34% of Swedes and 22% of Japanese. With regard to the idea that "we are headed for environmental disaster unless we change our habits quickly," only 57% of Americans agreed, compared with 84% percent of Italians.[17]

The traditional view of divine omnipotence has been held by a significant percentage of Americans, as polls have shown. For example, a 2012 Gallup poll indicated that 46% of the U.S. population holds that our world was created within the past 10,000 years[18]—a belief that implies an omnipotent creator. About half of the Americans holding that belief, which discourages belief that climate change results from human-caused global warming, are members of Evangelical Protestant churches. As a result, polls have shown, a significantly lower percentage of Evangelicals believe that climate change is caused by human activity than do Americans in general.[19]

These studies do not mean that theological belief is the only factor behind climate denial. They also do not mean that all Evangelicals deny climate science; some affirm it strongly.[20] What they do indicate is that the belief in divine omnipotence has given Evangelicals a strong tendency to deny climate science.

The opinion of Pope Francis could not be more different. Saying that destroying the environment is a "grave sin against God the creator,"[21] he indicated the same about climate-change denial, saying: "Obstructionist attitudes, even on the part of believers, can range from denial of the problem to indifference, nonchalant resignation or blind confidence in technical solutions" (LS 14).

THE FALSITY OF DIVINE OMNIPOTENCE

Insofar as society has thought of the world as created by an omnipotent deity, it has held a false view of God. This view can be called false because many false and harmful ideas have followed from it. Of the many facts that show this, five will be mentioned here.

First, the doctrine of divine omnipotence has led to an insoluble problem of evil, meaning the impossibility of reconciling divine omnipotence with the belief, essential to Christian faith, that God is good and loving. No satisfactory solution has been provided in the eighteen centuries since the doctrine of divine omnipotence was firmly accepted.

This acceptance occurred near the end of the second century A.D., when Christian theologians began affirming that the universe was created *ex nihilo* (out of nothing). They did this in reaction to the gnostic theologian Marcion, who declared that the world has so much evil because the God of the Hebrews had created the world out of evil matter. To forestall this idea, some Christian theologians, who were not especially astute philosophically, decided to declare that the world was not made of any matter whatsoever (whether good, evil, or neutral).[22]

This new Christian doctrine contradicted the idea, affirmed by both Plato and the book of Genesis, that our world was created out of chaos (rather than absolute nothingness), with the matter in a state of chaos being neither good nor bad but neutral. Plato taught that the world's creator willed that everything should be good "as far as possible." And the first verses of Genesis, when correctly translated, say: "When God began to create the heaven and the earth, the world was without form and void."[23] Both traditions said that God created our world out of something that had some power of its own.

By rejecting this view, which was held by Jews throughout the Old Testament period and by both Jews and Christians during most of the first two Christian centuries, the doctrine of *creatio ex nihilo* said that when God began to create our world, God was not confronted by any stuff with power of its own, with which the divine power could be resisted.

In the words of 20th-century Calvinist theologian Millard Erickson, "God did not work with something which was in existence. He brought into existence the very raw material which he employed." Otherwise, Erickson said, God would "have been limited by having to work with the intrinsic characteristics of the raw material which he employed." Accordingly, he said, "God's will is never frustrated. What he chooses to do, he accomplishes."[24]

That doctrine implies that all the terrible things in the world — including the genocide of native Americans, the slavery and lynching of American blacks, the Nazi Holocaust, the atomic bombings of Hiroshima and Nagasaki, and life-destroying diseases, such as cancer, AIDS, Alzheimer's, and the plague — have happened because God freely chose to cause them, or at best allowed them to happen while having the power to prevent them.

It is now widely believed that divine goodness cannot be reconciled with divine omnipotence. A strong inductive argument for this conclusion is provided by the fact that no satisfactory resolution has ever been provided.[25]

Second, the doctrine of divine omnipotence contradicts the scientific worldview, which presupposes that the universe involves a web of cause-and-effect relations that cannot be broken now and then.

Alfred North Whitehead described this worldview in his 1925 book, *Science and the Modern World.* The scientific mentality,

Whitehead said, "instinctively holds that all things great and small are conceivable as exemplifications of general principles which reign throughout the natural order," so that "every detailed occurrence can be correlated with its antecedents in a perfectly definite manner, exemplifying general principles."[26]

Although it has been common to say that the scientific worldview arose in the 17th century, with scientists such as Descartes, Boyle, and Newton being central, these men still allowed for occasional divine interventions in the natural cause-effect relations.[27] However, in the 19th century (even earlier in France), thinkers came to presuppose that, in the words of one German scholar at the time, "all things are linked together by a chain of causes and effects, which suffer no interruption."[28]

To be sure, many philosophers and theologians even today do not accept this view. For example, Millard Erickson says that, "while [nature] ordinarily functions in uniform and predictable ways in obedience to the laws he has structured into it, [God] can and does also act within it in ways which contravene these normal patterns (miracles)."[29] Likewise, according to American Calvinist philosopher Alvin Plantinga, "God often treated what he has made in a way different from the way in which he ordinarily treats it."[30] And British philosopher Richard Swinburne, saying that God can bring about "any event he chooses," explained that "God is not limited by the laws of nature; he makes them and can change or suspend them."[31]

These thinkers are thereby opposing the view that has become presupposed by the scientific community for at least the last century and a half. This now-presupposed view has led many scientists and science-based philosophers to reject belief in God, understood as entailing divine omnipotence. For example, Harvard biologist Richard Lewontin has written: "To appeal to an omnipotent deity is to allow that at any moment the regularities of nature may be ruptured, that miracles may happen."[32]

Third, the doctrine of divine omnipotence has also led many Christians to reject the idea that our world came about through a very long, slow, evolutionary process, in favor of the fundamentalist view that our universe was created only a few thousand years ago. According to a 2013 Pew Research poll, 33 percent of Americans hold that "humans and other living things have existed in their present form since the beginning of time."[33]

To reconcile this view with the fossil record, fundamentalist scholars argue that God, when creating the world *ex nihilo*, created it with apparent traces of previous existence that had never occurred. For example, a 19th-century Christian scholar argued that Adam had a navel, even though he was not born; that trees were created with rings; and that hippopotamuses were formed with worn-down teeth.[34] Likewise, a contemporary rabbi wrote:

> [T]he real age of the universe is 5755 years, but it has mis-leading evidence of greater age. The bones, artifacts, partially decayed radium, potassium-argon, uranium, the red-shifted light from space, etc.—all of it points to a greater age which nevertheless is not true.[35]

Such claims could not have arisen apart from the doctrine of *creatio ex nihilo*. The belief that the present state of the world came about through a long evolutionary process is based on so much evidence that it is now beyond reasonable doubt.[36]

Fourth, the rejection of climate science also counts as a clearly false belief, because between 95.5 and 99.8 percent of the climate scientists who have published peer-reviewed articles on the topic affirm the reality of human-caused global warming.[37] Like the rejection of evolution, the rejection of climate science depends on the belief in divine omnipotence based on the doctrine of *creatio ex nihilo*. The similar unscientific basis of these two rejections was illustrated in 1981, when the National Center for Science Education expanded its original mission—to defend the teaching of evolution—to "defending the teaching of evolution and climate science."[38]

Fifth, the doctrine of divine omnipotence has led traditional Christian theologians to think of Christianity as "the one true religion"[39] — a view that has now been increasingly rejected by Christian thinkers.[40] Like these thinkers, the pope does not portray Christianity as the only authentic and worthwhile religion. Rather, he speaks of *religions* (in the plural), encouraging "religions to dialogue among themselves for the sake of protecting nature, defending the poor, and building networks of respect and fraternity" (LS 143).

DIVINE POWER: POPE FRANCIS AND PROCESS THEOLOGY

Does Pope Francis hold the traditional doctrine of omnipotence, according to which the power of God could rupture the regularities of nature? Does he hold the view that human beings need not fear global warming because, if God does not want it to destroy human civilization, God can simply override any natural forces that could drive us toward extinction? This might seem to be implied by the pope's reference to God as "the all-powerful creator" (LS 246).

GOD AS ALL-POWERFUL: POPE FRANCIS

However, there is nothing in the pope's encyclical suggesting that he is complacent about climate change. To the contrary, the encyclical began with the statement that we are faced "with global environmental deterioration" (LS 3), in relation to which he quoted the statement of Pope Paul VI that, "Due to an ill-considered exploitation of nature, humanity runs the risk of destroying it and becoming in turn a victim of this degradation" (LS 4).

In the same vein, Pope Francis said in his address to the United Nations (as quoted above in the Introduction): "The ecological crisis, and the large-scale destruction of biodiversity, can threaten the very existence of the human species."[41] It would be hard for the pope to be much more non-complacent.

There is no suggestion that Pope Francis agrees with Senator Inhofe that, because "God is still up there," there is no basis for alarm. There is likewise no suggestion that the pope agrees with the claim of Congressman Shimkus that the "Earth will end only when

God declares it's time to be over." Like Rush Limbaugh, the pope knows that human beings are not omnipotent, but he does not agree with Limbaugh's assurance that we, therefore, could not "destroy the climate."

How, then, are we to interpret the pope's reference to God as the "all-powerful creator"? A clue is provided by his statement that the "universe did not emerge as the result of arbitrary omnipotence." Rather, the pope said, "Creation is of the order of love. God's love is the fundamental moving force in all created things" (LS 78).

This statement suggests that Pope Francis, like process theology, considers God's power to be the power of love. Perhaps the pope's strongest statement to this effect occurred in his discussion of the fact that various conditions can spawn "antisocial behavior and violence." He stated:

> I wish to insist that love always proves more powerful. Many people in these conditions are able to weave bonds of belonging and togetherness which convert overcrowding into an experience of community in which the walls of the ego are torn down and the barriers of selfishness overcome. (LS 149)

Rather than there being a conflict between divine power and divine love, Pope Francis appears to say that God's power consists of God's love, which is "the fundamental moving force in all created things."

GOD AS ALL-POWERFUL: PROCESS THEOLOGY

According to process theologians, God could be called "all-powerful creator," but not in the sense that God essentially has all the power, so that all creaturely power could be overridden. Rather, God is all-powerful in the sense of being the supreme power in reality. Having power that is qualitatively different from any other power, God has the unique power to bring forth a universe.[42]

As scientists have recently realized, the existence of our universe has depended on incredibly precise fine-tuning of the physical laws and constants of physics. Stephen Hawking wrote:

> The laws of science, as we know them at present, contain many fundamental numbers, like the size of the electric charge of the electron and the ratio of the masses of the proton and the electron.... The remarkable fact is that the values of these numbers seem to have been very finely adjusted to make possible the development of life.[43]

The evidence for the fine-tuning of the universe, along with reasons to consider it to be the doing of the creator of the universe, will be discussed more fully in Chapter 5. For now, the present chapter discusses the implications of fine-tuning for divine power.

FINE-TUNING AND DIVINE POWER

With regard to the attribute of being "uniquely powerful," theistic commentators often argue that the fine-tuning for life points to the existence of a deity who is omnipotent in the traditional sense.[44] Omnipotence in this traditional sense includes the power to cancel out, or override, the power of the creatures.

However, power in that sense is not entailed by the kind of power needed to fine-tune a universe. In fine-tuning, God would be dealing with what Whitehead called "eternal objects," which are mere possibilities, such as numbers, ratios, and shapes. God would, therefore, not be dealing with actual things, such as molecules, bacteria, brain cells, humans, mountains, and oceans. These actual things have power of their own, so their states and behaviors cannot be unilaterally determined by God.[45] In saying that God's power is not coercive, Whitehead meant that God does not overrule the power of the creatures. He said: "God's role is not the combat of productive force with productive force, of destructive force with destructive force."[46]

In addition to having that unique creative power, God is the one agent that is omnipresent, so that God has the unique power to influence all parts of the universe simultaneously. Taking this divine influence into account allows us to explain various things that otherwise remain mysterious. For example, said: "Why nature is mathematical is a mystery," said Nobel-Prize-winning physicist Richard Feynman, "a kind of miracle."[47] Physicist James Trefil, pointing out that "the laws of nature we discover here and now in our laboratories are true everywhere in the universe," calls this fact "astonishing."

In accounting for such otherwise unexplainable universal facts, Whitehead endorsed Plato's view of "a basic Psyche whose active grasp of ideas conditions impartially the whole process of the Universe."[48]

WORLD CREATED BY DIVINE DECISION

Quoting a verse in the Psalms, "By the word of the Lord the heavens were made" (Ps 33:6), the pope said: "This tells us that the world came about as the result of a decision" (LS 77). Process theology might seem to contradict this idea, given Whitehead's view that God and the World both presuppose the other.[49]

However, in saying that the World, like God, exists necessarily, Whitehead was referring to the idea that a realm of finite entities exists necessarily—not our particular world, to be sure, but simply *some* world or other. In referring to the World (with a capital "W"), he was saying that there is always a realm of finite entities.

Our particular world, by contrast, is what Whitehead calls a "cosmic epoch," with its contingent (arbitrary) laws of nature, such as the existence of electrons, protons, molecules, and star systems. "The arbitrary...elements in the laws of nature," he said, "warn us that we are in a special cosmic epoch."[50] A cosmic epoch, Whitehead explained, "may be, relatively to our powers, of immeasurable extent temporally and spatially. But in reference to the ultimate nature of things, it is a limited nexus."[51]

Accordingly, although the World is uncreated, existing eternally, our cosmic epoch, which is what is usually meant by speaking of "the world," has been created by God. That is, whereas the World as such continues to exist between cosmic epochs in a state of chaos, our particular world came about by virtue of God's bringing order out of chaos. In agreement with Plato, Whitehead said:

The creation of the world is the incoming of a type of order establishing a cosmic epoch. It is not the beginning of matter of fact, but the incoming of a certain type of order.[52]

The type of order establishing a cosmic epoch provides what we call the "laws of nature." Accordingly, God is the creator of our world because, in Whitehead's words, "'God' is that actuality in the world, in virtue of which there is physical 'law.'"[53] Because the laws of our cosmic epoch result from God's decision to instill these laws, the creation of our world resulted from a divine decision.

CREATION THROUGH LOVE

As noted above, Pope Francis, saying that the universe did not result from arbitrary omnipotence, said: "God's love is the fundamental moving force in all created things" (LS 77). How could the creation of the world result from divine love?

According to process theology, God's power is not the power to coerce creatures to obey the divine will. Rather, divine power is the power of love. The divine love, besides being compassion for all creatures, is also the power to create and transform.

God's power to create and transform operates persuasively, by means of offering attractive possibilities. What Whitehead calls God's "primordial nature" contains all pure possibilities, which he called "eternal objects," meaning all the possibilities that could be actualized in our or any other cosmic epoch. Sometimes, God offers *novel* eternal objects, meaning possibilities previously unrealized in our cosmic epoch. The acceptance of these novel possibilities lies behind the occurrence of evolution — from cosmic and geological evolution through the evolution of life and humanity. In Whitehead's words, "Apart from the intervention of God, there could be nothing new in the world."[54] In fact, Whitehead used the occurrence of novelty as one of the major reasons to affirm the reality of God.[55]

In providing new possibilities, God does so out of love — the desire to increase the capacity of creatures to experience higher forms of value. Whitehead said: "The consciousness which is individual in us, is universal in [God]; the love which is partial in us is all-embracing in him.... His purpose is quality of attainment."[56]

In addition to saying that God creates out of love, Pope Francis seems to hold a similar view of possibilities and novelty, saying: "The Spirit of God has filled the universe with possibilities and therefore, from the very heart of things, something new can always emerge" (LS 80).

CONCLUSION

It appears that there are remarkable similarities between the position of Pope Francis and that of the process thought based primarily on the philosophy of Alfred North Whitehead.

These similarities may reflect a common root: Whitehead and the pope were both influenced by Henri Bergson. Whitehead named Bergson one of the thinkers to whom he was "greatly indebted."[57] And Pope Francis was influenced by fellow Jesuit Pierre Teilhard de Chardin (see LS note 53) — as were Pope Benedict and Pope John Paul II before him. And Teilhard, like Whitehead, had been influenced by Bergson. Although Teilhard disagreed with Bergson about much, it was Bergson's *Creative Evolution* that inspired Teilhard to study evolution.[58]

In any case, the pope and process theology share the view that God created the world out of love, not omnipotence, so that God's being all-powerful does not entail that God could unilaterally prevent global warming from destroying civilization.

NOTES

1   Cindy Wooden, "Pope Francis Explains Why He Chose St. Francis of Assisi's Name," *Catholic News Service,* 17 March 2013.

2   Jack Wintz, O.F.M., "St. Francis of Assisi: Why He's the Patron of Ecology," St. Anthony Messenger Press, October 2007.

3   John B. Cobb, Jr., *Is It Too Late? A Theology of Ecology* (1972; Denton, TX: Environmental Ethics Books, 1995), 23.

4   Ibid., 65.

5   Leonora Cohen Rosenfield, *From Beast-Machine to Man-Machine: Animal Soul in French Letters from Descartes to La Mettrie,* 2nd ed. (London: Octagon Books, 1968); Steven Nadler, "Cartesianism and Port-Royal," *Monist,* 70 (1988), 570–84.

6   See Julius Adler and Wung-Wai Tso, "Decision-Making in Bacteria," *Science* 184 (1974):1292–94. On philosophy as well as science, see David Ray Griffin, *God Exists but Gawd Does Not* (Anoka, MN: Process Century Press, 2016), Chapters 4 and 13.

7   St. Augustine, *Enchiridion,* trans. J. F. Shaw, XIV.96; XVI.102; *The City of God,* trans. Marcus Dods, X.14.

8   John Calvin, *Institutes of the Christian Religion,* ed. John T. McNeill, trans. Ford Lewis Battles, 2 Vols. (Philadelphia: Westminster Press, 1960), 3.23.7; 1.18.1.

9   Martin Luther, *On the Bondage of the Will,* trans. J. I. Packer and O. R. Johnston (Grand Rapids, Mich.: Fleming H. Revell, 1957), 614–20. (These numbers refer to the numbering of the Weimar edition of Luther's works.)

10 Ibid., 634–39.

11 Senator James Inhofe, *The Greatest Hoax: How the Global Warming Conspiracy Threatens Your Future* (Washington, D.C.: WND Books, 2012), 70–71.

12 "God Won't Allow Global Warming, Congressman Seeking to Head Energy Committee Says," Raw Story, 11 November 2010.

13 David Edwards, "Limbaugh: Christians 'Cannot Believe in Man-made Global Warming,'" Raw Story, 14 August 2013.

14 "An Evangelical Declaration on Global Warming," Cornwall Alliance, 1 May 2009.

15 Meredith Bennett-Smith, "Calvin Beisner, Evangelical Christian, Claims Environmentalism Great Threat to Civilization," Huffington Post, 21 March 2013.

16 "Climate Change: Key Data Points from Pew Research," Pew Research Center, 2 April 2013; Max Fisher, "Americans Are Less

Worried about Climate Change than Almost Anyone Else," *Washington Post,* 27 September 2013.

17   Joanna M. Foster, "Poll: U.S. Leads the World...in Climate Denial," Climate Progress, 22 July 2014.

18   Frank Newport, "In U.S., 46% Hold Creationist View of Human Origins," Gallup, 1 June 2012.

19   Lauren Markoe, "On Evolution and Climate Change, Evangelicals Stand Apart According to Poll," Huffington Post, 22 September 2011; David C. Barker and David H. Bearce, "End-Times Theology, the Shadow of the Future, and Public Resistance to Addressing Global Climate Change," *Political Research Quarterly,* June 2013; Christopher Mooney, "New Study Reaffirms the Link between Conservative Religious Faith and Climate Change Doubt," *Washington Post,* 29 May 2015.

20   See David Ray Griffin, *Unprecedented: Can Civilization Survive the CO2 Crisis?* (Atlanta: Clarity Press, 2015), Chapter 11, "Climate Change Denial," which discusses Katherine Hayhoe and Richard Cizik; Coco McPherson, "God's Work: Meet the Woman Turning Evangelicals Into Environmentalists," *Rolling Stone,* 17 June 2015, which discusses Anna Jane Joyner; and Liz Schmitt, "Talking to Evangelicals about Climate Change," *Sojourners,* March 2014.

21   Peter Sinclair, "Pope Francis: Destroying Environment a 'Grave Sin,'" Climate Denial Crock of the Week, 31 October 2014.

22   Gerhard May, *Creatio Ex Nihilo: The Doctrine of "Creation out of Nothing" in Early Christian Thought,* translated by A. S. Worrall (Edinburgh: T. & T. Clark, 1994).

23   Plato, *The Timaeus,* 30A; Jon D. Levenson, *Creation and the Persistence of Evil: The Jewish Drama of Divine Omnipotence* (San Francisco: Harper & Row, 1988).

24   Millard J. Erickson, *Christian Theology* (Grand Rapids: Baker Book House, 1985), 374, 277.

25   I myself have provided much of this inductive argument by providing a critique of major philosophers and theologians who have tried: See David Ray Griffin, *God, Power, and Evil: A Process Theodicy* (1976; Louisville: Westminster John Knox, 2004); *Evil Revisited: Responses and Reconsiderations* (Albany: State University of

New York Press, 1991); "In Response to William Hasker," in John B. Cobb, Jr., and Clark H. Pinnock, eds., *Searching for an Adequate God: A Dialogue between Process and Free Will Theists* (Grand Rapids: Eerdmans, 2000); "Traditional Free Will Theodicy and Process Theodicy: Hasker's Claim for Parity," *Process Studies* 29/2 (Fall-Winter 2000); and my contributions to Stephen T. Davis, ed., *Encountering Evil: Live Options in Theodicy,* 2nd edition (Louisville: Westminster John Knox, 2001), 108–25.

26 Alfred North Whitehead, *Science and the Modern World* (1925; New York: Free Press, 1967), 5, 12.

27 See Chapter 5, "Religion and the Rise of the Modern Scientific Worldview," in David Ray Griffin, *Religion and Scientific Naturalism: Overcoming the Conflicts* (Albany: State University of New York Press, 2000).

28 David Friedrich Strauss, *The Life of Jesus Critically Examined,* trans. George Eliot (1855; Minneapolis: Fortress Press, 1972).

29 Millard J. Erickson, *Christian Theology* (Grand Rapids: Baker Book House, 1985), 54.

30 Alvin Plantinga, "Reply to the Basingers on Divine Omnipotence," *Process Studies* 11/1 (Spring 1991): 25–29.

31 Richard Swinburne, *Is There a God?* (Oxford University Press, 1996), 7.

32 Richard Lewontin, "Billions and Billions of Demons," *New York Review of Books,* 9 January 1997: 28–32, at 31.

33 "Public's Views on Human Evolution," Pew Research, 30 December 2013.

34 Ann Thwaite, *Glimpses of the Wonderful: The Life of Philip Henry Gosse, 1810–1888* (London: Faber & Faber, 2002), 209, 216.

35 Rabbi David Gottlieb, "The Age of the Universe" (http://www. dovidgottlieb.com/comments/AGEOFTHEUNIVERSE.htm).

36 See Eugenie C. Scott, *Evolution vs Creationism: An Introduction,* 2nd ed. (Westport, CT: Greenwood Press, 2009). Saying that evolution is beyond doubt does not entail, to be sure, that the neo-Darwinian view of evolution is true.

37 Peter T. Doran and Maggie Kendall Zimmerman, "Examining the Scientific Consensus on Climate Change," *Earth and Environmental*

Sciences 90/20 (20 January 2009); James Powell, "The State of Climate Science: A Thorough Review of the Scientific Literature on Global Warming," *Science Progress,* 15 November 2012.

38   "Anti-Evolution and Anti-Climate Science Legislation Scorecard: 2013," National Center for Science Education, 20 May 2013.

39   Christian theologians had traditionally argued that the Bible, understood as the inerrant word of God, teaches that Christianity is the one true religion; see Kathy LaPan, "Why Christianity is Exclusive: The Only True Religion," Religious Tolerance, 1 April 2013. It was long a dogma of the Roman Catholic Church that "there is no salvation outside the church"; see Michael Müller, "Extra Ecclesiam Nullus omnino Salvatur," The Catholic Dogma. For a recent example, Steven B. Cowan and James Spiegel, defending the "traditional, orthodox accounts of divine omnipotence," argued that "Christianity is exclusively true" (*The Love of Wisdom: A Christian Introduction to Philosophy* [B&H Publishing Group 2009], 314).

40   See John B. Cobb, Jr., *Beyond Dialogue: Toward a Mutual Transformation of Christianity and Buddhism* (Fortress Press, 1982); David Ray Griffin, ed., *Deep Religious Pluralism* (Westminster/John Knox, 2005); S. Mark Heim, *Salvations: Truth and Difference in Religion* (Maryknoll, NY: Orbis Books, 1995); John Hick, *A Christian Theology of Religions: The Rainbow of Faiths* (Louiseville: Westminster John Knox, 1995); Paul F. Knitter, *Jesus and the Other Names: Christian Mission and Global Responsibility* (Maryknoll, NY: Orbis Books, 1996); Knitter, ed., John B. Cobb Jr., *Transforming Christianity and the World: A Way beyond Absolutism and Relativism* (Maryknoll, NY: Orbis Books, 1999); Leonard Swidler, John B. Cobb Jr., Paul F. Knitter, and Monika K. Hellwig, *Death or Dialogue? From the Age of Monologue to the Age of Dialogue* (**City??:** SCM Press and Trinity Press, 1990).

41   Ryan Teague Beckwith, "Transcript: Read the Speech Pope Francis Gave to the United Nations," *Time,* 25 September 2015.

42   See David Ray Griffin, *God Exists but Gawd Does Not* (Anoka, MN: Process Century Press, 2016), Chapters 1, 13, and 14. The discussion below employs statements quoted in these chapters.

43   Stephen Hawking, *A Brief History of Time* (New York: Bantam Books, 1988), 125.

44 For example, George F. R. Ellis, "The Theology of the Anthropic Principle," in Robert J. Russell et al., eds., *Quantum Cosmology and the Laws of Nature: Scientific Perspectives on Divine Action* (Vatican: Vatican Observatory Publications & Berkeley: The Center for Theology and the Natural Sciences, 1993), 363–99; Richard Swinburne, "The Argument to God from Fine-Tuning Reassessed," in Neil A. Manson, ed., *God and Design: The Teleological Argument and Modern Science* (New York: Routledge, 2003), 80–105.

45 With regard to this list of actual things: Molecules, bacteria, brain cells, and humans, being true individuals, have the power to exert self-determination as well as the power to exert influence on other things, as discussed below in Chapter 6. But mountains and oceans, being things with aggregational order, have only the power to influence other things, not also the power to exert self-determination.

46 Whitehead, *Process and Reality,* originally published 1929; corrected edition, ed. David Ray Griffin and Donald W. Sherburne (New York: Free Press, 1978), 346.

47 Richard Feynman, *The Meaning of It All: Thoughts of a Citizen-Scientist* (New York: BasicBooks, 1998), 43.

48 Whitehead, *Adventures of Ideas* (1933; New York: Free Press, 1967), 147.

49 Whitehead, *Process and Reality,* 348.

50 Ibid., 64, 89.

51 Ibid., 288.

52 Ibid., 96.

53 Ibid., 283.

54 Ibid., 247. This was arguably an unfortunate statement by Whitehead, because the notion of "intervention" by God is widely used to refer to an "interventionist" deity, who occasionally interrupts the normal laws of nature. Whitehead of course did not mean this. He meant only that, unless God were always making novel possibilities available, novelty in the world would be impossible.

55 Johnson, A. H., "Whitehead as Teacher and Philosopher" *Philosophy and Phenomenological Research* 29 (1969), 351–76, at 367.

56 Whitehead, *Religion in the Making* (Macmillan, 1926 [reprint New

York: Fordham University Press, 1996]), 158–59.

57 Whitehead, *Process and Reality,* xii.

58 H. James Birx, "The Phenomenon of Pierre Teilhard de Chardin," The Harbinger, 27 May 1997.

CHAPTER TWO

False Morality

IN ADDITION TO HAVING A FALSE IDEA OF GOD, modern culture also has a false morality. This false morality is largely based on the false idea of God, or on a rejection of the idea of God altogether.

SCIENCE AND RELIGION

"[I]n the areas of politics and philosophy," said Pope Francis, "there are those who firmly reject the idea of a Creator, or consider it irrelevant." As a result, they ignore the contributions that can be made by the dialogue between science and religion (LS 62). "If we are truly concerned to develop an ecology capable of remedying the damage we have done," insisted the pope, "no branch of the sciences and no form of wisdom can be left out, and that includes religion" (LS 63).

Whitehead held a similar view. Pointing out that modern cosmology has been based almost entirely upon scientific ideas, in distinction from ideas rooted in aesthetic, ethical, and religious experience, Whitehead said that we need to retain "the whole of the evidence in shaping our cosmological scheme," including religious experience. Indeed, speaking of science and religion, Whitehead said that "it

31

is no exaggeration to say that the future course of history depends [upon our decision] as to the relations between them."[1]

RELATIVISM AND LACK OF CONCERN FOR FUTURE GENERATIONS

The rejection of a divine creator, said the pope, leads to a complete relativism, according to which "there are no indisputable truths to guide our lives, and hence human freedom is limitless." This relativism has led to the deterioration of the natural environment as well as the social environment (LS 6).

Whitehead, being in the tradition of Scottish commonsense philosophy, rejected the idea that there are no indisputable truths to guide our lives. Rather, he said that "we must bow to those presumptions, which, in despite of criticism, we still employ for the regulation of our lives. Such presumptions are imperative in experience."[2]

One of those presumptions, he maintained, is the existence of moral norms. Because "the impact of... moral notions is inescapable,"[3] we cannot have a rational position if we verbally deny any of "the moral intuitions which are presupposed in the concrete affairs of life."[4]

Also agreeing with the pope's view that morality is derived from God, Whitehead wrote:

> There are experiences of ideals — of ideals entertained, of ideals aimed at, of ideals achieved, of ideals defaced. This is the experience of the deity of the universe.[5]

In addition to modernity's *theoretical* relativism, the rejection of the reality of God also, said Pope Francis, has led to *practical* relativism derived from anthropocentrism, in which human beings place themselves in the center of existence. In this practical relativism, humans "give absolute priority to immediate convenience and all else becomes relative." Relativism in this sense "sees everything as irrelevant unless it serves one's own immediate interests" (LS 122).

This attitude, in which people become self-centered, increases their greed. "The emptier a person's heart is, the more he or she needs things to buy, own and consume" (LS 204). This greed, along with the focus on immediate interests, has led to "today's self-centered culture of instant gratification" (LS 162), which in turn has led to the ecological crisis.

"The pace of consumption, waste and environmental change has so stretched the planet's capacity that our contemporary lifestyle," said the pope, "can only precipitate catastrophes" (LS 161). It is difficult for us to take action with regard to this challenge, because of "an ethical and cultural decline which has accompanied the deterioration of the environment" (LS 162).

This ethical and cultural decline has tended to produce people with no "concern for the environment and the rights of future generations" (LS 109). This lack of concern for future generations is a symptom of the fact that today's culture has "[lost] sight of the great motivations which make it possible for us to... make sacrifices"—sacrifices motivated by a "sense of intergenerational solidarity" (LS 162, 200).

Behind the deterioration of nature and the unconcern for future generations—said the pope in a 2013 apostolic proclamation—"lurks a rejection of ethics and a rejection of God" (EG 57 [standing for *Evangelii Guadium*, paragraph 57]).

Losing sight of the great motivations that support concern for the future, Whitehead held, is an effect of the loss of a religious vision of reality—a loss that undermines the motivations that prevent cultural decline. "The vigour of civilized societies," he wrote, "is preserved by the wide-spread sense that high aims are worth-while."[6] This sense is created and sustained by "the intuition of the sacred, which is at the foundation of all religion." He continued:

> In every advancing civilization this sense of sacredness has found vigorous expression. It tends to retire into a recessive factor in experience, as each phase of civilization enters upon its decay.[7]

Hoping for a culture in which high aims can be sustained and thereby help the human race to survive, Whitehead said: "Philosophy should now perform its final service. It should seek the insight, dim though it be, to escape the wide wreckage of a race of beings sensitive to values beyond those of mere animal enjoyment."[8]

LACK OF CONCERN FOR THE COMMON GOOD

The failure to be concerned about future generations is closely related to the decline of the idea of the common good: "[O]ur inability to think seriously about future generations," said Pope Francis, "is linked to our inability to broaden the scope of our present interests" (LS 162).

The most articulated theme in the pope's two major writings — *Evangelii Gaudium* and *Laudato Si'* — is the centrality of the common good. Calling it "a central and unifying principle of social ethics," Pope Francis said that human ecology "is inseparable from the notion of the common good." All economic policies, he added, should be shaped by concerns for the "dignity of each human person and the pursuit of the common good" (EG 203).

The notion of the common good is central to the climate crisis, because the climate is the most crucial aspect of the global commons. The climate has now become the preeminent example of the "tragedy of the commons," which was made famous by Garrett Hardin.[9] The tragedy occurs when a resource that can be used by everyone is unregulated. Because it is useful but unregulated, many people, being concerned only for their own self-interest rather than the common good, use up the resource.

This tragedy is not unrelated to the increasing secularity of society. When the sense of the sacred is blocked out, Pope Francis suggested, "a genuine sense of the common good also disappears" (LS 204). Commitment to the common good is an expression of charity, or love, which affects not only relationships between individuals but also society. Accordingly, the pope said, "the Church set before the world the ideal of a 'civilization of love'" (LS 239). Today, however, the concern for the common good has been replaced by "the globalization of indifference" (LS 52). The notion of the common good, moreover, is not limited to the present:

The notion of the common good also extends to future generations. The global economic crises have made painfully obvious the detrimental effects of disregarding our common destiny, which cannot exclude those who come after us. . . . [T]he world we have received also belongs to those who will follow us. (LS 159)

The climate crisis illustrates dramatically that global society has moved away from this concern, because "[t]he climate is a common good, belonging to all and meant for all" (LS 23). The global summits about the climate have failed, because special economic interests "easily end up trumping the common good" (LS 54). Put otherwise:

International negotiations cannot make significant progress due to positions taken by countries which place their national interests above the global common good. (LS 169)

This self-centered concern for our own economy has been manifested in untold numbers of statements by American political leaders. For example, discussing the Kyoto agreement, which aimed to slow global warming, President George W. Bush said he could not sign the Kyoto agreement, because it "would have wrecked our economy."[10]

This attitude is clearly idolatrous, because it means valuing the short-term success of the American economy over the common good—which in this case means the survival of civilization. (Idolatry will be discussed in the following chapter.)

SPECIAL ATTENTION TO THE POOR

Against the globalization of indifference, the pope advocates an "integral ecology," based on his oft-repeated point that "everything is connected." The pope especially gives attention to the connection of the condition of the environment and that of the poor. Indeed, he says, "the gravest effects of all attacks on the environment are suffered by the poorest" (LS 48.) For example, "There has been a tragic rise in the number of migrants seeking to flee from the growing poverty caused by environmental degradation" (LS 25).

To give another example, one of the effects of climate change is an increase in drought in areas that had already been dry (whereas historically wet regions are now being subjected to deluges). "Water poverty," said Pope Francis, "especially affects Africa where large sectors of the population have no access to safe drinking water" (LS 28). In tune with his emphasis on "integral ecology," the pope said:

> Our world has a grave social debt towards the poor who lack access to drinking water, because they are denied the right to a life consistent with their inalienable dignity. (LS 30)

In perhaps the pope's clearest statement of "integral ecology," he said that the world needs "an integrated approach to combating poverty, restoring dignity to the excluded, and at the same time protecting nature" (LS 139). Phrased otherwise, a true ecological approach "must integrate questions of justice in debates on the environment, so as to hear both the cry of the earth and the cry of the poor" (LS 49).

This integral ecology includes an "economic ecology," which is necessarily "an integral part of the development process" (LS 114). Spelling out his vision more fully, Pope Francis said:

> We urgently need a humanism capable of bringing together the different fields of knowledge, including economics, in the service of a more integral and integrating vision. (LS 141)

This integral ecology gives special attention to the growing needs of the poor due to climate change, because "growing numbers of people are deprived of basic human rights." In this situation:

> [T]he principle of the common good immediately becomes, logically and inevitably, a summons to solidarity and a preferential option for the poorest of our brothers and sisters. (LS 158)

PROCESS THINKERS ON THE COMMON GOOD

Whitehead was very concerned with the revival of concern for the common good. Knowing that it would be futile to ask people to try to act contrary to their interests, Whitehead said that the goal should be to inculcate a worldview that would help people enlarge their interests: "The antithesis between the general good and the individual interest can be abolished only when the individual is such that its interest is the general good." [11] How could that be done?

The formation of such individuals requires a religion based on a deity with universal concerns. Religion, Whitehead said, "is directed to the end of stretching individual interest beyond its self-defeating particularity." [12] This effect can be realized, of course, only if the religion is oriented to an all-inclusive deity: "The consciousness which is individual in us, is universal in [God]: the love which is partial in us is all-embracing in him." [13] With this vision of deity, our fundamental religious drive—the desire to imitate deity (*imitatio dei*)—will inspire true moral goodness, the enlargement of our sympathies and interests.

The present culture, however, encourages people not to be concerned for the general good, but to be interested only in their self-centered interests. This is relevant to the climate, of course, because—to repeat the pope's observation: "The climate is a common good, belonging to all and meant for all" (LS 23).

Whitehead's concern with the common good is reflected in social-economic thought developed by process thinkers. In addition to being reflected in the title of the aforementioned book by John Cobb and economist Herman Daly, *For the Common Good*,[14] it is also reflected in Cobb's 1994 book *Sustaining the Common Good: A Christian Perspective on the Global Economy*.[15]

Cobb's fullest discussion of this notion is contained in a 2003 lecture, "Making Choices for the Common Good," in which he explained the basic idea:

> The very idea of the common good implies that we are bound together, that the good of one depends on the good of others and supports their good.[16]

Like Pope Francis, Cobb spoke of "the urgent need to revivify belief in the importance of caring for something beyond the interests of one's self and the groups with which one identifies." [17]

In explaining the need to "revivify" this belief, Cobb said: "Fifty years ago, this sense could be taken for granted in the sense that most Americans recognized that they should be concerned for 'the people of the nation as a whole, and, beyond that, 'the world as a whole.'" Cobb did not mean, to be sure, that most people actually organized their lives around these convictions, but only that "the basic Christian teaching that we should be concerned for others as well as for ourselves was taken for granted as normative."[18]

Today, however, Cobb continued, "as secularization has proceeded, the idea has lost ground." Many major philosophers, presupposing atheism, now say that, "if someone sees no reason to modify self-interested behavior for the benefit of others, philosophers can provide no reason why they should."[19] The Christian idea has been replaced by economic theory, which teaches that to act rationally is "to gain as much as possible while giving as little as possible in terms of money or labor."[20]

The concern for the common good also leads Cobb, like Pope Francis, to "call for a preferential option for the poor."[21]

To conclude: For modern culture in general, acting for the sake of the common good is no longer a widely shared ideal. This ideal will be revitalized only if the practice of taking economic theory as normative is replaced by a revitalized Christian faith or some other religion with similar effects. The decline of ethical concern for the common good and future generations is closely related, agree both Pope Francis and process thinkers, to the idolatry of money.

NOTES

1   Alfred North Whitehead, *Science and the Modern World* (1925; New York: Free Press, 1967), vii, 181.

2   Alfred North Whitehead, *Process and Reality,* corrected edition, ed. David Ray Griffin and Donald W. Sherburne (New York: Free Press, 1978), 151.

3   Whitehead, *Modes of Thought* (New York: Free Press, 1968), 19.

4 Whitehead, *Process and Reality,* 80.

5 Whitehead, *Modes of Thought,* 103.

6 Alfred North Whitehead, *Adventures of Ideas* (1933; New York: Free Press, 1967), 288.

7 Whitehead, *Modes of Thought,* 120.

8 Whitehead, *Adventures of Ideas,* 159.

9 Garrett Hardin, "The Tragedy of the Commons," *Science* 162 (December 1968), 1243–48.

10 "Bush: Kyoto Treaty Would Have Hurt Economy," *Associated Press,* 30 June 2005.

11 Whitehead, *Process and Reality,* 15.

12 Ibid., 15.

13 Alfred North Whitehead, *Religion in the Making* (Macmillan, 1926 [reprint New York: Fordham University Press, 1996]), 152.

14 Herman E. Daly and John B. Cobb, Jr., *For the Common Good: Redirecting the Economy Toward Community, Environment, and a Sustainable Future* (Boston: Beacon Press, 1989; rev. ed., 1994).

15 John B. Cobb, Jr., *Sustaining the Common Good: A Christian Perspective on the Global Economy* (Cleveland: Pilgrim Press, 1994).

16 John B. Cobb, Jr., "Making Choices for the Common Good" (lecture), Luther Northwestern Seminary, 21 September 2003.

17 Ibid.

18 Ibid.

19 For examples of the kinds of philosophers to whom Cobb is referring, see the discussions of John Mackie, Gilbert Harman, Bernard Williams, and Richard Rorty in Chapter 8, "Morality," in Griffin, *God Exists but Gawd Does Not* (Anoka, MN: Process Century Press, 2016).

20 Cobb, "Making Choices for the Common Good."

21 John B. Cobb, Jr., "The Theological Stake in Globalization," Center for Process Studies. See also Cobb's "Economism As Idolatry," Religion Online (www.religion-online.org/showarticle.asp?title=196).

CHAPTER THREE

Idolatry

CENTRAL TO THE REASONS why our culture has been destroying our home, said Pope Francis, is the fact that worship of the true God has been displaced by the worship of an idol: money. This critique echoes one that has been issued by process thinkers.

POPE FRANCIS: THE IDOLATRY OF MONEY

The worship of the golden calf described in Exodus 32, said the pope in *Evangelii Gaudium*, "has returned in a new and ruthless guise in the idolatry of money" (EG 55). In public talks, Pope Francis has said that the economic model based on the god of money not only "needs to sacrifice human lives on the altar of money and profit"; it also "needs to plunder nature to sustain the frenetic rhythm of consumption that is inherent to it."[1] Expressing even more fully the threat of this idolatry to nature, as well as the poor, the pope said:

> The thirst for power and possessions knows no limits. In this system, which tends to devour everything which stands in the way of increased profits, whatever is fragile, like the environment, is defenseless before the interests of a deified market, which become the only rule. (EG 56)

Describing this "deified market" in less theological terms, Pope Francis has condemned the "absolute autonomy of the marketplace and financial speculation" — an autonomy that results in a "new tyranny," which "relentlessly imposes its own laws and rules" (EG 56).

The pope's critique of the market has aroused antagonism, primarily involving the most profitable product in the market, fossil fuels. The continued use of these fuels, said Pope Francis, will result in "extraordinary climate change and an unprecedented destruction of ecosystems." Accordingly, the use of fossil fuels "needs to be progressively replaced without delay" (LS 165).

Behind the insistence on the autonomy of the market, said the pope in a statement quoted in the previous chapter, "lurks a rejection of ethics and a rejection of God." The true God is rejected, because "ethics leads to a God who calls for a committed response which is outside the categories of the marketplace." Calling for just this response, Pope Francis declared: "Money must serve, not rule!" (EG 57, 58) An ethical policy, he explained, must integrate justice and the environment, "so as to hear," as quoted in the previous chapter, "both the cry of the earth and the cry of the poor" (LS 49).

Neither of those cries can be addressed by relying on the market. Contrary to the claim that having a completely free market will help the poor, the pope denies "that economic growth, encouraged by a free market, will inevitably succeed in bringing about greater justice and inclusiveness in the world" (EG 54). Equally absurd, Pope Francis said, is the claim that the environment can best be protected by an unregulated market. Quoting a pontifical compendium of the church's social doctrine, he said:

> [E]nvironmental protection cannot be assured solely on the basis of financial calculations of costs and benefits. The environment is one of those goods that cannot be adequately safeguarded or promoted by market forces.

We must, the pope added, "reject a magical conception of the market, which would suggest that problems can be solved simply by an increase in the profits of companies or individuals" (LS 190).

Moreover, said the pope's encyclical, there needs to be a complete change in the model of global development:

> It is not enough to balance, in the medium term, the protection of nature with financial gain, or the preservation of the environment with progress. Halfway measures simply delay the inevitable disaster. (LS 194)

For an example of halfway measures, the encyclical could have quoted influential Yale economist William Nordhaus. Having long argued for the need to "balance costs and benefits,"[2] Nordhaus argued in a 2013 book that "good policies must lie somewhere between wrecking the economy and wrecking the world."[3] Besides falsely assuming that saving the world would necessarily harm the economy (rather than helping it, as some economists have been realizing), Nordhaus's statement suggests that saving the planet (for thousands of years) is no more important than saving the U.S. economy (for the present decade). The pope rightly says that that the kind of balance suggested by Nordhaus should be resisted.

In any case, rather than trying to balance the protection of nature against the present model of development, Pope Francis said, the world needs to redefine the notion of progress, saying: "A technological and economic development which does not leave in its wake a better world and an integrally higher quality of life cannot be considered progress" (LS 194).

The availability of drinking water provides an example of how the quality of life for many people has been undermined by the global economy. As the pope points out: "[A]ccess to safe drinkable water is a basic and universal human right, since it is essential to human survival and, as such, is a condition for the exercise of other human rights" (LS 30). Nevertheless, because governments have, while focusing on the economy, refused to stop global warming, the availability of fresh water has been shrinking.

Studies warn, moreover, that an acute water shortage is likely within a few decades, with repercussions for billions of people. Nevertheless, "in some places there is a growing tendency, despite [water's] scarcity, to privatize this resource, turning it into a commodity subject to the laws of the market" (LS 30, 31). Using a memorable metaphor for the greed that is destroying both human lives and the environment, the pope said:

> [B]ehind all this pain, death and destruction there is the stench of what Basil of Caesarea, one of the church's first theologians, called "the dung of the devil." An unfettered pursuit of money rules. That is the dung of the devil.

Because of this dung, added the pope:

> Our common home is being pillaged, laid waste and harmed with impunity. Cowardice in defending it is a grave sin. We see with growing disappointment how one international summit after another takes place without any significant result.[4]

PROCESS THINKERS ON IDOLATRY

Process thinkers have been criticizing what they call "growth idolatry" since John Cobb and economist Herman Daly discussed it in their 1977 book, *For the Common Good*.[5] Following theologian Paul Tillich, who said that idolatry occurs when "something essentially partial is boosted into universality," Cobb and Daly defined idolatry as "commit[ting] oneself finally to anything less than the whole."[6]

JOHN COBB ON ECONOMISM AS IDOLATRY

Speaking of the primary example of idolatry today, Cobb used the term "economism," defined as "the belief that primary devotion should be directed to the expansion of the economy." Just as Pope Francis said that the global economy is now based on the idolatry of money, Cobb said that economism is now the dominant religion, at least in the West. Economism had reached this status in the middle of the 20th century, Cobb added, when it replaced nationalism as the common ideology.[7]

This new ideology, Cobb explained, means a reversal of the relation between the nation and the market: "Whereas in nationalism the market serves the nation, in economism, nations are subordinated to the market."[8] Making the same critique, Pope Francis said: "Politics must not be subject to the economy" (LS 189).

Cobb was not alone, of course, in describing the real religion of the modern world as oriented around money. Already in 1957, Karl Polanyi's classic study *The Great Transformation* described capitalism as a new universal religion, with a new theology.[9] In 1995, Canadian economist Rodney Dobell wrote:

> The hegemony achieved by this particular intellectual construct—a "European religion" or economic religion—is remarkable; it has become a dogma of almost universal application, the dominant religion of our time, shoring up and justifying what would appear to be a patently inequitable status quo.[10]

The "market value system," in the words of Canadian philosopher John McMurtry, constitutes a "new world religion," or a "new world theology," which functions as the "deifier of the ruling order."[11]

Accordingly, Cobb's criticism of economism as the new dominant religion is, like the pope's criticism of money idolatry, in line with previous critiques.

HERMAN DALY ON GROWTH IDOLATRY

Cobb's sometimes co-author Herman Daly has focused on the destructive idea of endless economic growth. In providing an alternative, Daly has advocated a steady-state economy. Daly's thinking about this was developed originally in response to the famous 1972 book *The Limits to Growth*[12] (sponsored by the Club of Rome, which was founded to "rebel against the suicidal ignorance of the human condition"[13]). By "limits to growth," the authors of this book did not mean that there could be no increase in most dimensions of growth, such as growth in intelligence, morality, and beauty. They simply

meant that quantitative biophysical growth could not continue forever, because the planet if finite.

A book arguing that there are limits to growth was necessary,
because the economic world had failed to adjust to the realization that
the planet's resources are finite. When modern economic thought was
created centuries ago, the human economy was tiny in relation to
nature, with its vast resources. Economic ideas were developed on
the assumption that human industry would never be able to use up
the planet's resources, that it would never be able to harm the ocean
or the atmosphere. It was assumed, therefore, that economic growth
could continue forever. *The Limits to Growth* argued that this was
no longer true.

Although this fact should have been self-evident, the reaction
from the economic community was vitriolic. A *Newsweek* editorial
by Yale economist Henry Wallich called the book "irresponsible nonsense." Wilfred Beckerman, writing in the *Oxford Economic Review*,
said the book was "such a brazen, impudent piece of nonsense that
nobody could possibly take it seriously." Julian Simon and Herman
Kahn said that it was rightly "damned as foolishness or fraud by
every serious economic critic." And the science editor of *Forbes* called
the book "as wrong-headed as it is possible to be." [14]

As fervent believers in unending economic growth, these writers
treated *The Limits to Growth* as religious heresy. These critics were
set off primarily by the first of the book's two concluding points,
which stated:

> 1. If the present growth trends in world population, industrializa-
> tion, pollution, food production, and resource depletion continue
> unchanged, the limits to growth on this planet will be reached
> sometime. The most probable result will be a rather sudden and
> uncontrollable decline in both population and industrial capacity.

More precisely, the book's prediction was that if such growth continued to the point where "global equilibrium" could not be achieved,
the collapse would occur "within the next one hundred years."

Mainstream economists, however, generally criticized the book as if it had prophesized that this decline would be reached by 2000.[15] Also, they ignored almost entirely the book's second concluding point, which was the authors' main reason for writing the book:

> 2. It is possible to alter these growth trends and to establish a condition of ecological and economic stability that is sustainable far into the future. The state of global equilibrium could be designed so that the basic material needs of each person on earth are satisfied and each person has an equal opportunity to realize his individual human potential.[16]

Ignoring this hopeful prospect, mainstream economists, still focusing on the first point, continued denouncing the book. Two decades after the book's publication, William Nordhaus argued that to follow the book's recommendations would "send humanity back to the living standards of the Dark Ages." By contrast, Nordhaus assured readers, "an efficiently managed economy need not fear shipwreck on the reefs of resource exhaustion or environmental collapse."[17]

However, here we are, within only the fifth decade after publication of *The Limits of Growth*, fearing both resource exhaustion and environmental collapse before the end of the present century. Knowledgeable people now say that the book was largely accurate.[18]

Herman Daly was the one important economist at the time who took seriously the book's argument about the need for equilibrium. Indeed, his 1977 book, *Steady-State Economics*, was subtitled *The Economics of Biophysical Equilibrium and Moral Growth*.[19] John Stuart Mill, the main founder of steady-state economics, had defined it as "a stationary condition of capital and population" — which did *not* imply a "stationary state of human improvement."[20]

In explaining a steady-state economy, Daly defined it thus:

> An economy with constant population and constant stock of capital, maintained by a low rate of throughput that is within the regenerative and assimilative capacities of the ecosystem.[21]

A steady-state economy, added Daly, is an alternative to "growth mania." Explaining the meaning of this term sardonically, Daly wrote:

> Economic growth is held to be the cure for poverty, unemployment, debt repayment, inflation, balance-of-payment deficits, pollution, depletion, the population explosion, crime, divorce, and drug addition. In short, economic growth is both the panacea and the *summum bonum*. This is growthmania. When we add to GNP the costs of defending ourselves against the unwanted consequences of growth and happily count that as further growth, we then have hyper-growthmania. When we deplete geological capital and ecological life-support systems and count that depletion as net current income, we arrive at our present state of terminal hyper-growthmania.[22]

In criticizing growthmania, Daly was not necessarily rejecting economic growth as such. Rather, he came to focus on "uneconomic growth," which is growth that "impoverishes rather than enriches." It impoverishes, because additional GNP "would increase costs more than it increased benefits." Mainstream economists, said Daly, "assume that welfare is positively correlated with activity so that increasing GNP will increase welfare." But now, continued Daly,

> growth is becoming uneconomic. Uneconomic growth will not sustain the demographic transition and cure overpopulation. Neither will it help redress unjust distribution, nor cure unemployment. Nor will it provide extra wealth to be devoted to environmental repair and cleanup.[23]

Arguing against the "irrational commitment to exponential growth forever on a finite planet," Daly said that society must "overcome the growth idolatry."[24]

Pope Francis understood this point completely, criticizing "the idea of infinite or unlimited growth, which proves so attractive to economists, financiers and experts in technology." This idea, said the pope, is "based on the lie that there is an infinite supply of the earth's goods" (LS 109).

Growth idolatry is illustrated by a statement made by Larry Summers when he was the treasury secretary in the Clinton administration. He declared:

> [The government] cannot and will not accept any 'speed limit' on American economic growth. It is the task of economic policy to grow the economy as rapidly sustainably, and inclusively as possible.[25]

Daly's case against "uneconomic growth" is echoed by Pope Francis. Directly after the pope's statement quoted above about the notion of progress—that "economic development which does not leave in its wake a better world and an integrally higher quality of life cannot be considered progress"—he said:

> Frequently, in fact, people's quality of life actually diminishes—by the deterioration of the environment, the low quality of food or the depletion of resources—in the midst of economic growth. (LS 194)

STEADY-STATE ECONOMICS AND ECONOMIC DEGROWTH

A contemporary movement influenced by Daly, along with his former professor Nicholas Georgescu-Roegen, is known as "economic degrowth." The term "degrowth" is, most people agree, unattractive, but like most words, it sounds nicer in French, "décroissance."[26]

In any case, it is not possible to describe *the* relation between degrowth and Daly's steady-state economics, because members of the degrowth movement have quite different views. For example, some members, such as Georgescu-Roegen himself, see them as opposed on important issues. But others regard the ideals as complementary and helpful, as long as neither is literalized. For example, Christian Kerschner and Giorgos Kallis say: On the one hand, there cannot be a literally steady-state economy, as Georgescu-Roegen says, but Daly's goal is sensible and possible if it is understood as a *quasi*-steady-state economy. On the other hand, economies could not literally keep degrowing forever. Rather, wealthy countries should degrow until they get down to the state in which they are sustainable for a very long time. Both steady-state and degrowth movements agree that civilization will not be sustainable unless there is radical degrowth in wealthy countries.[27]

In addition to this similarity between the degrowth movement and Daly and Cobb's process thinking, Barbara Muraca pointed out—in a contribution to Cobb's edited volume, *For Our Common Home: Process-Relational Responses to Laudato Si'*—that the pope's encyclical holds the same view. In fact, she quoted the above-quoted statement by Pope Francis about economic growth—that people's quality of life frequently diminishes in the midst of economic growth because of ecological deterioration.[28]

CONCLUSION

We will not be able to save our common, sacred home unless our society overcomes its idolatrous devotion to money, especially to economic growth. Far from continuing to "grow the economy," rich countries need to *degrow the economy* until it gets down to the point at which a steady-state economy will be sustainable, given the planet's finitude. The need for degrowth is illustrated by the fact that today, "humanity uses the equivalent of 1.5 planets to provide the resources we use and absorb our waste," and that "if current population and consumption trends continue, by the 2030s, we will need the equivalent of two Earths to support us."[29]

The world is well on the way to proving the truth of the worst scenario warned against by *The Limits to Growth*. This scenario cannot be avoided unless we overcome the idolatry criticized by Pope Francis and process thinkers.

NOTES

1   Quoted in John Vidal, "Pope Francis's Edict on Climate Change Will Anger Deniers and US Churches," *Guardian,* 27 December 2014.

2   William D. Nordhaus, *A Question of Balance: Weighing the Options on Global Warming Policies* (New Haven: Yale University Press, 2008), 1–2.

3   William D. Nordhaus, *Climate Casino: Risk, Uncertainty, and Economics for a Warming World* (New Haven: Yale University Press, 2013), 176.

4   Daniel Burke, "Pope Calls Greed 'The Devil's Dung,'" CNN, 11 July 2015.

5   Herman E. Daly and John B. Cobb, Jr., *For the Common Good: Redirecting the Economy toward Community, the Environment, and a Sustainable Future* (1989), updated and expanded ed. (Boston: Beacon Press, 1994).

6   Paul Tillich, *Systematic Theology,* Vol. 1 (Chicago: University of Chicago Press, 1951), 13; Daly and John B. Cobb, *For the Common Good,* 389.

7   John B. Cobb, Jr., *The Earthist Challenge to Economism: A Theological Critique of the World Bank* (London: Macmillan, 1999), 13–28.

8   Ibid., 44.

9   Karl Polanyi, *The Great Transformation* (Boston: Beacon Press, 1957), 130, 133.

10   Rodney Dobell, "Environmental Degradation and the Religion of the Market," in Harold Coward, ed., *Population, Consumption, and the Environment* (Albany: State University of New York Press, 1995).

11   John McMurtry, *Unequal Freedoms: The Global Market as an Ethical System* (West Hartford, CT: Kumarian Press, 1998), 16; *The Cancer Stage of Capitalism* (London: Pluto Press, 1999), 14, 22-23.

12   Donella H. Meadows, Dennis L. Meadows, Jorgen Randers, and William W. Behrens III, *Limits to Growth* (New York: Signet, 1972).

13   Christian Parenti, "'The Limits to Growth': A Book That Launched a Movement," *The Nation,* 5 December 2012.

14   Henry Wallich, *Newsweek,* 13 March 1972; Wilfred Beckerman, "Economists, Scientists and Environmental Catastrophe," *Oxford Economic Papers,* 24/3 (1972); Julian Simon and Herman Kahn, *The Resourceful Earth: A Response to Global 2000* (Oxford: Basil Blackwell, 1984), 38; Ronald Bailey, "Dr. Doom," *Forbes,* 16 October 1989.

15   Matthew Simmons, "Revisiting The Limits to Growth: Could the Club of Rome Have Been Correct, After All?" *Energy Bulletin, 2000* (http://www.energybulletin.net/node/1512).

16   The Limits to Growth: Abstract Established by Eduard Pestel. A Report to The Club of Rome (1972), by Donella H. Meadows, Dennis l. Meadows, Jorgen Randers, William W. Behrens III."

17   William D. Nordhaus, "Lethal Model 2: The Limits to Growth Revisited," *Brookings Institute,* 1992.

18   Simmons, "Revisiting The Limits to Growth"; Jorgen Stig Norgard et al., "The History of The Limits to Growth," *Solutions,* February 2010; Christian Parenti, "'The Limits to Growth': A Book That Launched a Movement."

19   Herman E. Daly, *Steady-State Economics: The Economics of Biophysical Equilibrium and Moral Growth* (San Francisco, G.H. Freeman, 1977); 2nd ed. with new essays, Washington, D.C.: Island Press, 1991).

20   John Stuart Mill, *Principles of Political Economy* (Boston: Charles C. Little and James Brown, 1848).

21   Herman E. Daly, "A Steady-State Economy," Sustainable Development Commission, 2008; quoted by Peter Victor, "Herman Daly and the Steady State Economy," *The Herman Daly Festschrift* (Encyclopedia of Earth, 2013).

22   Herman E. Daly, "The Steady-State Economy: Postmodern Alternative to Growthmania," David Ray Griffin, ed., in *Spirituality and Society: Postmodern Visions* (Albany: State University at New York Press, 1988), 107–22, at 110.

23   Herman E. Daly, "Uneconomic Growth: Conflicting Paradigms," Acceptance Speech, Right Livelihood Award, 9 December 1996.

24   Herman E. Daly, "Climate Policy: From 'Know How' to 'Do Now,'" Keynote Address on Federal Climate Policy, American Meteorological Society, 4 September 2008.

25   Bill McKibben, *Eaarth: Making a Life on a Tough New Planet* (New York: Times Books, 2010), 47. The Summers statement was quoted in Robert M. Collins, *More: The Politics of Economic Growth in Postwar America* (New York: Oxford University Press, 2000), 8.

26   See Barbara Muraca, "Décroissance: A Project for a Radical

Transformation of Society," *Environmental Values* 22 (2013): 147–69; see also Panos Petridis, Barbara Muraca, Giorgos Kallis, "Degrowth: Between a Scientific Concept and a Slogan for a Social Movement," in Joan Martínez-Alier and Roldan Muradian, eds., *Handbook of Ecological Economics* (Cheltenham, UK: Edward Elgar, 2015).

27 See Christian Kerschner, "Economic De-Growth vs. Steady-State Economy," Institut de Ciència y Tecnologia Ambientals, 10 November 2009; Giorgos Kallis, "The Degrowth Alternative," The Great Transition Initiative, February 2015.

28 Barbara Muraca, "Care for Our Common Home and the Degrowth Movement: A Message of Radical Transformation," in John B. Cobb and Ignacio Castuera, eds., *For Our Common Home: Process-Relational Responses to Laudato Si'* (Anoka, MN: Process Century Press, 2015), 139–49.

29 "World Footprint," Global Footprint Network, 2015 (http://www.footprintnetwork.org/en/index.php/GFN/page/world_footprint/).

PART TWO

Reconstruction to Save Our Sacred Home

CHAPTER FOUR

Nature as Sacred

CLOSELY RELATED TO IDOLATRY as explaining why we are destroying our common home is the fact that the view of nature as sacred has declined. In some circles, it has completely disappeared.

In some traditional Christian circles, the idea of the natural world as sacred is considered a pagan idea, from which Christian faith should be completely separated. According to Christianity of this type, the world is not sacred; only God is. The only part of the created world that should be treated as sacred is humanity, because humans have been uniquely created in the image of God, and God was incarnated in Jesus. According to this view, nature has no intrinsic value. Its value is purely instrumental, having been created by God for the sake of human beings. Besides not being sacred, the world is not even of ultimate instrumental value, because God, being omnipotent, could simply replace the present world with "a new heaven and a new earth."

In atheist circles, nature is not sacred, because nothing is. Nature is not important because created by God, since God does not exist. This view easily leads to nihilism, according to which there is nothing of ultimate importance, and there are no moral norms in the fabric of the universe, such as the norm that we should protect the planet for future generations.

A third view is pantheism, according to which the universe as a whole is sacred. Pantheists regard the world with the same reverence that Christians, Jews, and Muslims have for God. On this basis, pantheists may be motivated to protect nature, but there is no moral injunction to do so, because pantheism holds that literally everything is equally divine. Pantheism, therefore, provides no basis for distinguishing between "is" and "ought"—between what is the case and what ought to be the case. There is, accordingly, no basis for saying that we should protect nature for future generations: The universe is sacred no matter what happens.

However, there is a fourth view, known as panentheism (pan-en-theism), according to which God is distinct from the universe, understood as the totality of finite things. But the universe in that sense is *in* God. What is sacred, then, is God-with-the-world. The world, accordingly, is sacred, but not in pantheism's sense, which obliterates the distinction between *is* and *ought* and hence the basis for moral norms. Panentheism, as distinct from pantheism, says that the creatures have their own power, with which they can act contrary to the divine will.

This is the view of process theology, and the present chapter suggests that the view of Pope Francis is closer to this fourth view than to any of the others.

THE SACREDNESS OF NATURE

In seeking to inspire fellow Christians to take care of the Earth as a common home, Pope Francis said:

> Everything is related, and we human beings are united as brothers and sisters on a wonderful pilgrimage, woven together by the love God has for each of his creatures and which also unites us in fond affection with brother sun, sister moon, brother river and mother earth. (LS 70)

But the pope also suggested that human beings will not become sufficiently motivated to save the Earth unless they regard it as sacred: "This common home of all men and women," he said in his address to the United Nations, "must also be built on the understanding of a certain sacredness of created nature."[1] Elsewhere, Pope Francis said: "The ideal is not only to discover the action of God in the soul, but also to discover God in all things" (LS 233).

How could the pope regard nature as sacred? How could he say that God is in all things? At least part of the pope's answer seems to be that the natural world has intrinsic value because it has experience.

NATURE AS HAVING INTRINSIC VALUE

Contrary to the view that only human beings have intrinsic value, Pope Francis said that we should not think of the various species merely as resources to be exploited, because all species "have value in themselves" (LS 33). Criticizing modernity's "excessive anthropocentrism," according to which the world was simply created for us, he said that *all* creatures "have an intrinsic value independent of their usefulness" (LS 140). Accordingly, "because every creature, particularly a living creature, has an intrinsic value," declared the pope, "a true 'right of the environment' does exist." He made this statement in the speech to the United Nations in which he spoke of "a certain sacredness of created nature."[2]

The pope's point of view could not be considered credible within the framework of the late modern worldview, according to which nature is composed, in Whitehead's critical words, "of an irreducible brute matter [that is] senseless, valueless, purposeless," because the ultimate entities of nature have "no intrinsic reality."[3] According to this view, the ultimate entities have no intrinsic value, because they have no experience.

Although Whitehead's words were written over 90 years ago, the view he was criticizing is still the dominant view in philosophy and science, which was the view articulated by Descartes in the 17th century. Asserting that nothing in creation except human minds had any experience, Descartes provided a rationale for a completely anthropocentric worldview. For example, as mentioned in Chapter 1, he and his followers argued that canine vivisection was not immoral, because dogs are simply machines, and, as such cannot feel pain.

By contrast, explaining why the conception of morals arises, Whitehead said: "We have no right to deface the value experience which is the very essence of the universe." In characterizing value experience, he added: "Its basic expression is — Have a care, here is something that matters!"[4] Following Descartes, modernity has said that — with the possible exception of human beings — we do not have to "have a care" with regard to anything, because there is nothing that matters.

BEYOND DESCARTES

Of course, it has been obvious to most people that dogs and other mammals have experience. Nevertheless, most people have also believed that a line must be drawn somewhere, below which there is no experience, merely insentient matter.

For example, well-known philosopher of science Adolf Grünbaum, writing in the 1960s, suspected that the line was roughly at the level of cockroaches, about which he was agnostic.[5] In the following decades, however, scientists started providing strong evidence that animal minds go down much further than previously thought. For example, professor of animal behavior Donald A. Griffin said that the dance of the honeybee, which transmits information about the location of food sources, "is not something the bees do mechanically and automatically," but instead involves thinking.[6]

Moreover, scientists have shown that even the most elementary living organisms are not devoid of experience. Already in the 1970s, microbiologists began reporting that bacteria — the lowest forms of life — make decisions based on experience. For example, a 1974 article was entitled "Decision-Making in Bacteria."[7] By now, many such studies have been published. Asking "How Do Bacteria Make Decisions?" a 2014 article said:

> Decision making is not limited to animals like humans or birds. Bacteria also make decisions with intricate precision.... If these bacteria are motile (able to move around), they can compare how conditions are for them now against how they were a few seconds ago. That's right, bacteria have a memory albeit short.[8]

The most famous evolutionary scientist making this case was Lynn Margulis. Speaking of "the perceptive capacity of all live beings,"[9] she said: "Bacteria are conscious. These bacterial beings have been around since the origin of life."[10]

BEYOND THE MIND-BODY PROBLEM

This discovery provides the basis for a solution to the major problem of modern philosophy, known as "the mind-body problem." The question is how the mind, with its experience, is related to the brain, composed of brain cells (neurons). Given the view, in line with Descartes's worldview, that our brain cells, like all other types of matter, are devoid of experience, it seemed impossible to understand how these material things could produce our conscious experience. It seemed equally impossible to explain how our consciousness could influence our brain cells, so that we can move our bodies.

One of our best philosophers, Thomas Nagel of New York University, explained the problem by using the French distinction between a *pour soi*, meaning an entity that is something "for itself" because it has experience, and an *en soi*, meaning something that is merely "in itself" because it has no experience. Nagel said:

> One cannot derive a *pour soi* from an *en soi*.... This gap is logically unbridgeable. If a [deity] wanted to create a conscious being, he could not expect to do it by combining

together in organic form a lot of particles with none but physical properties.[11]

Philosopher Colin McGinn, while agreeing with Nagel on this point, added that a neuron is *en soi,* devoid of experience. He wrote:

> How is it possible for conscious states to depend upon brain states?... How could the aggregation of millions of individually insentient neurons generate subjective awareness?... [W]e have no understanding of how consciousness could emerge from an aggregation of non-conscious elements.[12]

Discussing the emergence of consciousness in a fetus, McGinn said:

> [T]he human sperm and ovum are not capable of consciousness, and it takes a few months before the human fetus is. So when consciousness finally dawns in a developing organism it does not stem from an immediately prior consciousness: it stems from oblivion, from insensate (though living) matter.[13]

Descartes himself had dealt with this problem by saying that God, being omnipotent, coordinated the motions of our bodies, including our brains, with our conscious experiences. Although this appeal to divine omnipotence is no longer in fashion, some philosophers still make it, such as Oxford University's Richard Swinburne. Saying that "conscious men could not have evolved from unconscious matter by natural processes," because there is "no natural connection between brain-events and correlated mental events," Swinburne said that the otherwise mysterious mind-body connection can be explained by the agency of God, understood as "an omnipotent, omniscient, perfectly free and perfectly good source of all."[14]

McGinn agreed that Swinburne's position would seem to provide the only possible solution, saying:

> One is tempted, however reluctantly, to turn to divine assistance: for only a kind of miracle could produce this from

that. It would take a supernatural magician to extract consciousness from matter, even living matter.

Nevertheless, McGinn said, this kind of argument is no longer acceptable. He concluded, therefore, that the mind-body problem could never be solved—that it will forever remain a permanent mystery.[15]

However, this centuries-old problem no longer need stump philosophers. Neurons are eukaryotic cells, which are much more complex and sophisticated than prokaryotic cells. Evolutionarily, the emergence of prokaryotic cells emerged more than a billion years before eukaryotic calls appeared.[16] Bacteria are prokaryotic cells. If they have experience, then surely the same is true of the more complex eukaryotic cells that are our brain cells. Accordingly, contrary to McGinn, the experience of the fetus does not stem "from oblivion"—that is, from insensate matter—but from the developing brain cells, with their more primitive experience, just as the brain cells emerged from bacteria, with their still more primitive experience. In the words of Lynn Margulis, "Live small cells reside inside the larger cells."[17]

This is Thomas Nagel's solution. Saying that we need "a naturalistic expansion of evolutionary theory to account for consciousness,"[18] he says that we need a way to understand how we "descended from bacteria." This is possible, he says, by thinking of cells—both prokaryotic and eukaryotic—as "something more than physical," as "organisms with mental life."[19] Lynn Margulis said:

> Thought and behavior in people are rendered far less mysterious when we realize that choice and sensitivity are already exquisitely developed in the microbial cells that became our ancestors.[20]

It would seem that this view should be held by Pope Francis, since he surely does not think of God as—to use McGinn's term—a "supernatural magician." Indeed, the pope has said that God should not be imagined as "a magician, with a magic wand able to do everything."[21]

INTRINSIC VALUE ALL THE WAY DOWN

The recent developments in biology have gone far to support the pope's rejection of anthropocentrism in favor of saying that all creatures "have an intrinsic value independent of their usefulness." However, even if people can now agree that all living things, even bacteria, have experience and hence intrinsic value, the conventional view has been that experience could not possibly exist below the level of life. Below that level, it has been generally assumed, the entities must be devoid of experience and hence intrinsic value.

However, although the idea that non-living matter is devoid of experience has long been considered common sense, this idea prevents a self-consistent philosophy. If the organelles of which the bacterium is composed are completely devoid of experience, then we still have a "mind-body problem," only at a lower level. How could insensate organelles contribute to, and be influenced by, the experiencing bacterium as a whole?

This problem would not arise, of course, if organelles have a still lower level of experience. Some biologists now presuppose this, as illustrated by the above-quoted article about bacteria, which refers to "decision-making at a subcellular level," which would mean organelles. If organelles make decisions, they are not devoid of experience.[22]

But we would still have a "mind-body problem" if the macro-molecules of which the organelles are comprised are completely insentient. The solution is to reject the whole idea of a line between experiencing and non-experiencing entities.

This doctrine is called "panpsychism" or "panexperientialism." Whitehead developed his version of it in the 1920s, calling his position "the philosophy of organism." Explaining the name, he spoke of complex organisms as "organisms of organisms." Then, saying that electrons and hydrogen nuclei are quite elementary organisms, he specified that atoms and molecules are organisms of a higher type, with "individual living beings" being still more complex organisms.[23]

Endorsing Whitehead's position on this issue, Nagel said that we must think of natural entities as "something more than physical all the way down."[24] Speaking even more explicitly, Nagel said that we should, with Whitehead, regard "concrete entities, all the way down to the level of electrons," as having experience.[25]

Today a growing number of mainstream philosophers, in addition to Nagel, are taking this view.[26] As the Wikipedia article on "Panpsychism" said, the recent interest in the problem of consciousness "has once again made panpsychism a mainstream theory."[27] If this is the position of Pope Francis, he has a very up-to-date philosophy of nature.

WHITEHEAD ON INTRINSIC VALUE, GOD, AND THE SACRED

In light of Whitehead's view that all things have experience, the pope's statement affirming the presence of "God in all things" can be considered intelligible. In fact, Whitehead said: "Every event on its finer side introduces God into the world.... The world lives by its incarnation of God in itself."[28]

Although this statement might be considered merely metaphorical, Whitehead meant it more literally. According to his philosophy, when something is perceived most fundamentally, it does not remain merely external to the perceiver, as in sensory perception. Rather, there is a deeper mode of perception, which Whitehead called "prehension," in which the object, while remaining external, is also prehended into the perceiver. This is true of our prehension of anything in our environment. God, being omnipresent (as discussed in the following chapter), is in the environment of all creatures, so God is prehended by all creatures, entering into all of them.

Whitehead's position on the incarnation of God in all things is closely related to his sense of the sacred. Saying that the intrinsic reality of an event is best described as "value,"[29] Whitehead said that when "our sense of the value of the details for the totality dawns upon our consciousness," this is "the intuition of holiness, the intuition of the sacred, which is at the foundation of all religion."[30] Speaking of God as the "unity in the universe," Whitehead said: "There is a unity in the universe, enjoying value and (by its immanence) sharing value." In other words, the sense of the sacred is related to the intuition that we receive value from God and in turn contribute value to God.[31]

PANENTHEISM: WHITEHEAD AND POPE FRANCIS

Our world can also be called sacred because it exists in God. Charles Hartshorne, the major process philosopher after Whitehead, used the term "panentheism" for his position.[32] Describing God as "the soul of the universe,"[33] Hartshorne regarded all finite things as existing in God, analogously to the way the brain exists in the mind.

Although Whitehead himself did not use the word *panentheism*, Hartshorne said that it was the best term for his position. In fact, in response to the question whether it is "possible to indicate God's locus," Whitehead said:

> [I]n respect to the world, God is everywhere. Yet he is a distinct entity. The world (events in it) has a (specific) locus with reference to him, but he has no locus with reference to the world. This is the basis of the distinction between finite and infinite. God and the world have the same locus.[34]

Phrased otherwise, "panentheism" is the best term for Whitehead's position, because he held that all events in the world are prehended by, and thereby included in, the divine experience—which Whitehead called the "consequent nature of God." In affirming the two sides of panentheism, Whitehead said: "It is as true to say that the World is immanent in God, as that God is immanent in the World."[35] Whitehead affirmed, moreover, that this double immanence meant the double love of God: Referring to God's consequent nature as "the love in heaven," he also said that this love "floods back again into the world."[36]

Although Pope Francis has not used the term "panentheism," he expressed a similar position. Besides saying that "God [is] in all things" (LS 233), the pope also said that "the universe unfolds in God" (LS 91); he also described God as "the Creator who lives among us and surrounds us" (LS 155). "Even the fleeting life of the least of beings," he said, "is the object of his love, and in its few seconds of existence, God enfolds it with his affection" (LS 77).

Because of such passages, some writers have commented on the panentheistic flavor of the pope's encyclical. A writer in the Religion News Service suggested that the most radical part of the encyclical may be its "overall spiritual attitude toward nature," which the writer characterizes as "mystical nature panentheism."[37] Another writer has pointed out that the pope's position is in line with Ignatius of Loyola's *Spiritual Exercises*, which said:

> Consider how God dwells in creatures; in the elements, giving them existence; in the plants, giving them life; in the animals, giving them sensation; in human beings, giving them intelligence.... [God] is working in the heavens, elements, plants, fruits, cattle, and all the rest — giving them their existence, conserving them, concurring with their vegetative and sensitive activities, and so forth.

This writer then commented: "Though Ignatius may not have had a contemporary panentheistic cosmology in mind, his spirituality affirmed a pansacramental cosmology that allows for the manifestation of God in all things."[38]

CONCLUSION

In describing the world as sacred, Pope Francis said not only that God created our world, but also that all creatures have value in themselves and that God is present in all creatures. He equally said that all creatures are in God. Modern people may dismiss these statements as false, or as true only symbolically. This chapter shows, however, that the pope's statements, besides being in line with Ignatian spirituality, are supported by process theology, which in turn is supported by recent science. Part of the importance of this fact will be shown in Chapter 6, which explains why the evils in our world—including the threat of climate change to destroy civilization—do not contradict the assertions about the power and love of God.

NOTES

1   "The Address of Pope Francis to the United Nations."

2   Ibid.

3   Alfred North Whitehead, *Science and the Modern World* (1925; New York: Free Press, 1967), 17.

4   Alfred North Whitehead, *Modes of Thought* (1938; New York: Free Press, 1968), 116.

5   Adolf Grünbaum, "The Anisotropy of Time," in Thomas Gold, ed., *The Nature of Time* (Ithaca, NY: Cornell University Press, 1967), 149–86, at 152, 179–80.

6   Donald R. Griffin, *Animal Minds* (Chicago: University of Chicago Press, 1992), 182.

7   Julius Adler and Wung-Wai Tso, "Decision-Making in Bacteria," *Science* 184 (1974):1292–94.

8   Kim McDonald, "Bacteria Provide New Insights into Human Decision Making," UC San Diego, 8 December 2009; "Bacteria Use Chat to Play the 'Prisoner's Dilemma' Game in Deciding Their Fate," *American Chemical Society,* 27 May 2012); Matthew Russell, "How Do Bacteria Make Decisions?" Frontiers, 23 January 2014.

9   Lynn Margulis, "Gaia and Machines," in John B. Cobb, Jr., *Back to Darwin: A Richer Account of Evolution* (Grand Rapids, MI: Eerdmans, 2007), 167–75, at 172.

10   Dick Teresi, "Lynn Margulis Says She's Not Controversial, She's Right," *Discover Magazine,* April 2011.

11   Thomas Nagel, *Mortal Questions* (Cambridge: Cambridge University Press, 1979), 189.

12   Colin McGinn, *The Problem of Consciousness: Essays Toward a*

Resolution (Oxford: Basil Blackwell, 1991), 1, 213.

13   Ibid., 46.

14   Richard Swinburne, *The Existence of God* (Oxford: Clarendon, 1979), 161, 171–72; Swinburne, *The Evolution of the Soul* (Clarendon, 1986), 198–99.

15   McGinn, *The Problem of Consciousness,* 17n., 46.

16   "The Origin and Evolution of Cells," a chapter in Geoffrey M. Cooper and Robert E. Hausman, *The Cell: A Molecular Approach,* 2nd Edition (http://www.ncbi.nlm.nih.gov/books/NBK9841/).

17   Lynn Margulis, "Gaia Is a Tough Bitch," Chap. 7 of John Brockman, *The Third Culture: Beyond the Scientific Revolution* (New York: Simon & Schuster, 1995.

18   Thomas Nagel, *Mind and Cosmos: Why the Materialist Neo-Darwinian Conception of Nature Is Almost Certainly False* (Oxford and New York: Oxford University Press, 2012), 48.

19   Ibid., 30, 34, 53, 57.

20   Margulis, "Gaia Is a Tough Bitch."

21   Travis Gettys, "'God Is Not a Magician': Pope Says Christians Should Believe in Evolution and Big Bang," Raw Story, 28 October 2014.

22   Matthew Russell, "How Do Bacteria Make Decisions?" Frontiers, 23 January 2014.

23   Whitehead, *Science and the Modern World,* 110.

24   Nagel, *Mind and Cosmos,* 30, 34, 53, 57.

25   Ibid., 33.

26   Philosophers who advocate panpsychism include Michael Blamauer of the University of Vienna, David Chalmers of the University of California at Santa Cruz, D. S. Clarke of Southern Illinois University at Carbondale, William Seager of the University of Toronto at Scarborough, David Skrbina of the University of Michigan at Dearborn, and Galen Strawson of the University of Texas at Austin. Also, see *Panpsychism: Contemporary Perspectives,* ed. Godehard Brüntrup and Ludwig Jaskolla (Oxford University Press, 2016).

27   "Panpsychism," Wikipedia, accessed January 2015. Philosophers

who had made panpsychism a somewhat mainstream theory in earlier times included Wilhelm Gottfried Leibniz, Henri Bergson, Herman Lotze, William James, and Charles Peirce, while scientists included Charles Birch, David Bohm, Bernard Rensch, C. H. Waddington, and Sewall Wright (all of these scientists had essays in John B. Cobb, Jr., and David Ray Griffin, eds., *Mind in Nature: Essays on the Interface of Science and Philosophy* [Lanham, MD: University Press of America, 1977]).

28   Alfred North Whitehead, *Religion in the Making* (New York: Macmillan, 1926 [reprint New York: Fordham University Press, 1996]), 149.

29   Ibid., 97; Alfred North Whitehead, *Science and the Modern World*, 94.

30   Whitehead, *Modes of Thought*, 120.

31   Ibid., 119–20.

32   Charles Hartshorne and William L. Reese, eds., *Philosophers Speak of God* (Chicago: University of Chicago Press, 1953), 273–85,

33   Hartshorne, *Omnipotence and Other Theological Mistakes* (Albany, NY: State University of New York Press, 1984), 52–62.

34   A. H. Johnson, "Whitehead as Teacher and Philosopher," *Philosophy and Phenomenological Research* 29 (1969): 351–76, at 372.

35   Alfred North Whitehead, *Process and Reality,* corrected edition, ed. David Ray Griffin and Donald W. Sherburne (New York: Free Press, 1978), 348.

36   Ibid., 351.

37   Jay Michaelson, "Pope Francis' Environmental Encyclical Is even More Radical than It Appears," Religion News Service, 19 June 2015.

38   Hans Gustafson, "Pope Francis' Ignatian Tradition and Interfaith Relations," State of Affirmation, 2 April 2013.

CHAPTER FIVE

Evolution as Sacred

CONTINUING THE THEME OF THE PREVIOUS CHAPTER, the present chapter differs by focusing on the evolutionary process through which our present world emerged, showing why it should be considered sacred. This chapter, however, does not say much about the writings of Pope Francis: In neither the encyclical nor *Evangelii Gaudium* did he discuss evolution—except for indicating that he accepts biological evolution.[1] Elsewhere, however, he made clear his view, saying: "Evolution in nature is not inconsistent with the notion of creation, because evolution requires the creation of beings that evolve."[2] Also, explicitly rejecting the idea that the creation of the universe occurred without evolution, the pope said (in a statement partly quoted in the previous chapter): "When we read about Creation in Genesis, we run the risk of imagining God was a magician, with a magic wand able to do everything—but that is not so."[3]

In any case, rather than comparing the pope's views with those of process theology, this chapter deals with major stages of evolution—cosmic, geological, prebiological, biological, and human—through which present-day humanity emerged. These

71

stages are discussed for two purposes: To show why the whole evolutionary process should be considered sacred; and to prepare for
explaining in Chapter 6 why the horrible evils of our world do not
contradict the judgment that it is sacred.

EVOLUTION WORKS SLOWLY

Our world has been billions of years in the making. The creation of
our universe occurred—according to the dominant theory—somewhat over 13 billion years ago. Then about 4.5 bya (billion years ago),
the Earth was created. Our planet then underwent prebiological
evolution for about a billion years, during which self-replicating
organic molecules emerged. The most elementary forms of life (prokaryotic cells) emerged about 3.5 bya. Roughly another 1.5 billion
years passed before the emergence of the kinds of cells (eukaryotic)
that form plant and animal bodies (this was about 2 billion bya).
Almost another billion years passed before the emergence of multi-
cellular organisms (about 1.2 bya), after which roughly another half
billion years of evolution occurred before, about 500 mya (million
years ago), the so-called Cambrian Explosion, during which most
of the modern types of animals appeared.

The evolutionary process through which our world developed,
accordingly, was a very long, slow process. How did this process
result in life?

THE UNIVERSE WAS FINE-TUNED FOR LIFE

Lawrence Joseph Henderson, who taught biochemistry early in
the 20th century, wrote a book in 1913 entitled *The Fitness of the
Environment*, in which he called the universe "biocentric." In a subsequent book, entitled *The Order of Nature*, Henderson discussed properties that were preconditions of life, saying: "The chance that this
unique ensemble of properties should occur by 'accident' is almost
infinitely small."[4] Alfred North Whitehead, who cited both books

in *Process and Reality,* called them "fundamental for any discussion of [the order of nature]."[5]

In the 1970s, physicists started discussing the idea that the universe seemed to have been fine-tuned for life because of a large number of "coincidences," without which life could not have emerged. To give three examples:

- Gravity is extremely weak—about a trillion, trillion, trillion times weaker than electromagnetism. But if it had been still weaker, the stars would not have been hot enough to support planets on which life could develop. And if gravity had been a little stronger, the stars would have been so hot they would not have lasted long enough for the emergence of life on any planet.

- The strong force within the atom's nucleus, which binds protons and neutrons together, determines the amount of energy released when simple atoms undergo nuclear fusion. When hydrogen in a star turns into helium, the helium atom is slightly lighter than the two protons and two neutrons that went into making it. So 0.007 of the hydrogen's mass is converted into energy. But "no carbon-based biosphere could exist if this number had been 0.006 or 0.008 rather than 0.007."[6]

- Neutrons are slightly heavier than protons: The ratio of their masses is 939.56563 to 938.27231. If the mass of neutrons were increased a little, hydrogen could not be turned into helium, so stars could not be formed. But if neutrons were slightly lighter, there would be nothing but helium.[7]

The idea that the universe has been fine-tuned for life is now almost universally agreed, even by atheists. For example, Stephen Hawking said that "if the electric charge of the electron had been only slightly different, stars either would have been unable to burn hydrogen and helium, or else they would not have exploded."[8] The only question is about how to explain this fine-tuning.

EXPLAINING THE FINE-TUNING

The most obvious explanation would be that it was the work of the universe's creator: "It seems as though someone has fine tuned nature's numbers to make the universe," said astrophysicist Paul Davies. "The impression of design is overwhelming."[9]

Even some erstwhile atheists have accepted divine design of fine-tuning. For example, astronomer Fred Hoyle had long been so opposed to theism that he rejected the Big Bang—the name of which he had sarcastically coined—in favor of the steady-state view of the universe, because it seemed less suggestive of theism. But his atheism was "shaken," said Hoyle, by his study of the carbon nucleus.[10] This nucleus, he discovered, was formed from three helium atoms in a process that seemed so improbable that he was led to conclude:

> Some supercalculating intellect must have designed the prop-
> erties of the carbon atom.... The numbers one calculates
> from the facts seem to me so overwhelming as to put this
> conclusion almost beyond question.[11]

However, scientists not willing to give up atheism came up with another explanation: Assume that our universe is only one universe within a "multiverse" of billions and billions of universes, each with different laws of nature. In that framework, the argument goes, one of them was bound, purely by chance, to be like ours, with its fine-tuned variables. This hypothesis, they say, shows that the fine-tuning of our universe is compatible with atheism.

This explanation was endorsed by Stephen Hawking, who said: "The many improbable occurrences that conspired to enable our existence" would seem to be a miracle created by a benevolent God, "if ours were the only solar system in the universe." However, "the multiverse concept can explain the fine-tuning of physical law," he said, "without the need for a benevolent creator."[12]

Although the multiverse idea has been accepted by several scientists, other scientists have raised serious, seemingly fatal, criticisms of this idea. Here are five such criticisms:

- One problem with the multiverse hypothesis is that it is not based on any scientific evidence, but merely on the desire to avoid a creator. As Nobel Prize-winning scientist Arno Penzias said: "Some people are uncomfortable with the purposefully created world. To come up with things that contradict purpose, they tend to speculate about things they haven't seen."[13]

- It is widely thought that the multiverse hypothesis, by getting rid of the hypothesis of a divine creator, is superior by virtue of being a scientific hypothesis, as illustrated by an article entitled "Science's Alternative to an Intelligent Creator: The Multiverse Theory."[14] However, as deity-averse philosopher Thomas Nagel pointed out, "it is just as irrational to be influenced in one's beliefs by the hope that God does not exist as by the hope that God does exist."[15]

- Occam's razor says that, if all other things are equal, the simplest hypothesis should be chosen. By contrast, said Paul Davies, "the multiverse represents an inconceivably flagrant violation of Occam's razor—postulating an enormous ensemble of essentially unobservable universes, just to explain our own."[16]

- Referring to the widely accepted idea that science differs from speculative philosophical principles by virtue of being falsifiable, Paul Steinhardt—who had been one of the creators of the multiverse idea—said: "It's not even a scientific theory," because "it allows every conceivable possibility." Accordingly, there is no way either to verify or falsify the hypothesis.[17]

- A fifth problem is that the multiverse hypothesis does not really eliminate fine-tuning. "[T]he scientific multiple worlds hypothesis merely shifts the problem up a level from universe to multiverse," said Paul Davies. And according to Paul Steinhardt, although the whole idea was to eliminate fine-tuning, the multiverse hypothesis does not do this.[18]

Given these and still more problems,[19] it seems that the fine-tuning of the universe provides a very strong argument for the alternative explanation—that our universe was formed under the guidance of a very wise, omnipresent, and uniquely powerful agent.

DID A CREATOR NEED TO BE OMNIPOTENT?

Among philosophers and theologians who regard fine-tuning as due to a purposive creator, many of them believe that the creator is *omnipotent*, in the sense of having the ability completely to control the movements of all things in the universe.[20] However, there is no good reason to draw that conclusion.

For one thing, the notion of an omnipotent creator leads to the problem of evil, which either contradicts the idea of a divine creator or else requires one that is not good. For example, philosopher Quentin Smith argued that, given the enormous amount of evil in the universe, the fine-tuning of the universe leads to this conclusion: "If any spirit created the universe, it is malevolent, not benevolent."[21]

Also, the idea that only an omnipotent deity could fine-tune the universe is contradicted by the example of Alfred North Whitehead, who, before turning to speculative philosophy, was an applied mathematician working on problems in the philosophy of nature, such as quantum and relativity theory. Whitehead accepted the early version of fine-tuning developed by Lawrence Joseph Henderson while strongly rejecting the idea of divine omnipotence.

CONCLUSION

Without saying that God is omnipotent, we can say that God is responsible for setting up the basic laws of this universe, which made possible the evolution of the kind of universe we have. We can say, therefore, that the evolution of our universe is a sacred process.

THE EVOLUTION OF HUMANITY AND CIVILIZATION

As stated above, most of the modern types of plants and animals appeared in the Cambrian Explosion. Here is a very sketchy timeline of the major stages of the evolution of animals from the Cambrian Explosion to the emergence of human civilization:

MAJOR STAGES OF POST-CAMBRIAN ANIMAL EVOLUTION

- Mammals emerged about 220 million years ago (mya).

- Primates diverged from other mammals about 75 mya.

- Hominids or "great apes" emerged about 14 mya.

- Hominins, which include Australopithecines, chimpanzees, and humans, emerged about 8 mya.

- Humans, in the sense of the genus *Homo,* emerged about 2.5 mya.

- Modern humans (Homo sapiens) emerged about 500,000 years ago.

- Humans who are fully human physiologically (Homo sapiens sapiens) emerged about 200,000 years ago.

- Humans that are fully human behaviorally, with features such as language and music, emerged about 50,000 years ago.

- Finally, civilization, with the transition from hunter-gatherer societies to permanent settlements and agriculture, emerged about 10,000 years ago — a transition that was enabled by the emergence about 12,000 years ago of the Holocene era, in which the climate was warm enough for civilization to develop.

- More complex civilizations arose about 3,000 years ago.[22]

- Finally, a great evolutionary change in human consciousness arose in the so-called "axial age," about 500 years BCE, in various civilizations, including India, China, Greece, and Israel.[23]

Accordingly, just as the emergence of the Earth came after many billions of years of cosmic evolution, the emergences of life, mammals, human beings, human civilization, and today's human existence were also very long, slow processes.

A DIVINELY INSPIRED PROCESS

Given an evolutionary picture of our universe, the crucial question is, after the emergence of life: How can we account for the evolution from bacteria to today's human beings? In particular, "Why has the trend of evolution been upwards?"

This question, Whitehead pointed out, is not explained by the doctrine of the "survival of the fittest." This doctrine only explains why some organisms, having emerged, manage to survive. How did new forms of life first emerge?

"[T]he material universe has contained," Whitehead said, "some mysterious impulse for its energy to run upwards."[24] This mysterious impulse, he added, reflects "the purpose of God," which is "the attainment of value."[25] That is, whereas all organisms have some value, there are higher and lower forms of value, and God has inspired the universe with "a three-fold urge: (i) to live, (ii) to live well, (iii) to live better"—with the third of these meaning "to acquire an increase in satisfaction."[26]

The evolutionary process, insofar as it exemplifies an upward trend, requires—as discussed in Chapter 1—the actualization of novel possibilities, meaning ones that had never been realized in this world before. Referring to God as the *ground of novelty*,[27] Whitehead said that God answers the question, "where does novelty come from?"[28] Accordingly, novel forms derived from God, he said, "are the foundations of progress."[29]

Moreover, the emergence of homo sapiens sapiens, with their unique capacities—including those for higher mathematics, logic, rationality, and complex music (such as that of Bach, Mozart, and Beethoven)—cannot be explained as simply features of biological evolution. Rather, those capacities involve the actualization of possibilities that had never been exemplified before in this cosmic epoch, at least on our planet. Where were these possibilities during the billions of years before they were actualized by creatures in our world? Whitehead's answer is that they existed in what he called "the primordial nature of God."[30]

CONCLUSION

Because the evolutionary process was made possible by God's fine-tuning of the universe, and then by the divinely inspired upward trend of the evolutionary process — which leads to new modes of existence that can enjoy increasingly higher values — the entire process can be called sacred.

NOTES

1   The pope indicates this acceptance with his positive reference to Teilhard (LS note 53) and a comment referring to "the naturally slow pace of biological evolution" (LS 18).

2   Travis Gettys, "'God Is Not a Magician': Pope Says Christians Should Believe in Evolution and Big Bang," Raw Story, 28 October 2014.

3   Ibid.

4   Lawrence Joseph Henderson, *The Fitness of the Environment: An Inquiry into the Biological Significance of the Properties of Matter* (New York: Macmillan, 1913), 312; *The Order of Nature* (Cambridge, MA: Harvard University Press, 1917), 191.

5   Alfred North Whitehead, *Process and Reality,* corrected edition, ed. David Ray Griffin and Donald W. Sherburne (New York: Free Press, 1978), 89 n2.

6   Martin Rees, *Just Six Numbers: The Deep Forces that Shape the Universe* (New York: Basic Books, 2000), 54-57.

7   Oliver Sacks, "My Periodic Table," *New York Times,* 24 July 2015; Paul Davies, *The Goldilocks Enigma: Why Is the Universe Just Right for Life?* (Mariner Books, 2006), 141–43.

8   Stephen Hawking, *A Brief History of Time* (New York: Bantam, 1998), 129.

9   Paul Davies, *The Cosmic Blueprint* (New York: Simon & Schuster, 1988), 203.

10   Robin Collins, "The Evidence for Fine-Tuning," in Neil A. Manson, ed., *God and Design: The Teleological Argument and Modern Science* (New York: Routledge, 2003), 178–99, at 184.

11   Sir Fred Hoyle, "The Universe: Past and Present Reflections," *Engineering and Science,* November 1981.

12   Stephen Hawking and Leonard Mlodinow, *The Grand Design* (New York: Bantam, 2012), 153, 165.

13   Denis Brian, *Genius Talk: Conversations with Nobel Scientists and Other Luminaries* (New York: Plenum Press, 1995), 164.

14   "Science's Alternative to an Intelligent Creator: The Multiverse Theory," *Discover,* December 2008.

15   Thomas Nagel, *Mind and Cosmos: Why the Materialist Neo-Darwinian Conception of Nature Is Almost Certainly False* (Oxford and New York: Oxford University Press, 2012), 131.

16   Paul Davies, *Cosmic Jackpot: Why Our Universe is Just Right for Life* (Boston: Houghton-Mifflin Co., 2007), 179–85.

17   Maggie McKee, "Ingenious: Paul J. Steinhardt," *Nautilus,* 25 September 2014.

18   John Horgan, "Physicist Paul Steinhardt Slams Inflation, Cosmic Theory He Helped Conceive," *Scientific American,* 1 December 2014.

19   See Chapter 14, "Teleological Order," in Griffin, *God Exists but Gawd Does Not* (Anoka, MN: Process Century Press, 2016).

20   For example, Richard Swinburne, "The Argument to God from Fine-Tuning Reassessed" (80–105), and Robin Collins, "The Evidence for Fine-Tuning" (178–99), both in Neil A. Manson, ed., *God and Design: The Teleological Argument and Modern Science* (New York: Routledge, 2003).

21   Quentin Smith, "The Anthropic Coincidences, Evil and the Disconfirmation of Theism," *Religious Studies,* 1992.

22 For the approximate dates for this and the previous developments, one can see Wikipedia and other articles online.

23 Karl Jaspers, *The Origin and Goal of History* (New Haven: Yale University Press, 1953), 1–21; Lewis Mumford, *The Transformations of Man* (New York: Harper & Bros, 1967), Ch. 4; John B. Cobb, Jr., *The Structure of Christian Existence* (Philadelphia: Westminster Press, 1967), 52–59.

24 Alfred North Whitehead, *The Function of Reason* (1929; Boston: Beacon Press, 1968), 24.

25 Whitehead, *Process and Reality*, 244.

26 Whitehead, *The Function of Reason*, 4, 8.

27 Whitehead, *Process and Reality*, 67, 88.

28 William E. Hocking, "Whitehead as I Knew Him," in *Alfred North Whitehead: Essays on His Philosophy*, ed. by George L. Kline (Englewood Cliffs: Prentice-Hall, 1963), 7–17.

29 Ibid., 247.

30 Whitehead, *Process and Reality*, 46.

CHAPTER SIX

Evil and Sacredness

To think of the universe in general, and our planet in particular, as sacred is to believe that it is rooted in a reality that is holy or sacred. In Christianity and other theistic religions, this is expressed by saying that the universe was created by God, who is perfect.

However, the world's evil, as discussed in Chapter 1, is widely thought to contradict this view. Many people now believe that the universe is not rooted in a creator, or else that its creator is either evil or indifferent to the world's welfare.

THE PROBLEM OF EVIL

The conclusion that the world is not sacred, because not rooted in a good creator, is justified with respect to traditional theism, with its doctrine that the divine reality is omnipotent, capable of determining everything in the world.

This conclusion is most obviously true with regard to the classical version of traditional theism, according to which God actually determines every detail of the world—not only the physical world, with its earthquakes, tornadoes, and hurricanes, but also the movements of people's hearts. In the word's of St. Augustine, the wills of evil people "are so entirely at the disposal of God, that He turns them whithersoever He wills, and whensoever He wills." Accordingly, Augustine said, God "does in the hearts of even wicked men whatsoever He wills."[1]

But the conclusion that God is responsible for the world's evils is true also of the free-will version of traditional theism. It holds that, although God has the power to determine all of our actions, God allows us to have freedom, because otherwise we could neither be praised nor blamed for our actions; the distinction between virtue and vice would thereby be meaningless. Because humans are given genuine freedom, they, rather than God, are responsible for moral evil. But this allowance for human freedom does not keep God from being indictable for evil.

According to this free-will version of traditional theism, human freedom exists only as a gift of God. Therefore, God could override it at any time. In the words of one theologian:

> [E]ven though [God] bestowed relative independence on his creatures, as Creator he reserved the right to intervene if necessary. Thus he is able not only to permit human actions to occur, but also to prevent them from occurring if he so chooses.

Thereby, concluded this theologian, God "remain[s] in complete control."[2]

According to this theology, God would be able to prevent actions that would cause especially horrible evils, such as the murder of a saint, the rape of a child, or a holocaust (such as the Armenian or Nazi holocaust or that of Native Americans). This raises the question of why God would consider some evils important enough to prevent, but not these. This question has led many thoughtful people to atheism.

Some theologians avoid this question by holding that God, while able to intervene, never in fact does so, because God has made an irrevocable decision not to intervene. God made this decision never to intervene because the possession of freedom belongs to the essence of being human. Having us be fully human all of the time is so important to God, according to this view, that God never intervenes, no matter what. For example, if God had interrupted Hitler's plan to kill millions of people, God would have thereby violated Hitler's freedom and hence his full humanity.

Probably most people would say, however, that this would have been a small price to pay to prevent Hitler from violating the freedom and humanity of millions of other people. Indeed, Jewish theologian Richard Rubenstein wrote a book entitled *After Auschwitz,* in which he argued that no Jews after the Holocaust should believe in a God who could control the course of history.[3]

Moreover, even if God were thought to be justified in having made an irrevocable decision never to override human freedom, God would still be responsible for all the world's *natural* evils. These natural evils include the fact that our planet is susceptible to earthquakes, tornadoes, and hurricanes; the fact that human beings and other animals are susceptible to cancer and other diseases; and the fact that the Earth contains the elements to produce nuclear weapons and other weapons of mass destruction. The doctrine of *creatio ex nihilo* implies that God could have created a world supportive of human life without these dangers.

For example, a pacifist Christian theologian, worried during the Cold War about the threat of a nuclear holocaust, wrote a book with a chapter asking, "Why the Possibility for the Bomb?" He said:

> God certainly could have created the universe and the earth without uranium and thus without the possibility of these technological breakthroughs that have given human beings the capability of turning the planet into an uninhabitable waste. . . . God set us in the midst of a creation which contained that very hidden and most terrible possibility. Why? — when He could so easily have withheld it from us.[4]

The same question, given that theological perspective, can be asked about why the Earth was created with a combination of elements through which global warming can extinguish the human race along with the other higher forms of life.

FROM EVIL TO NIHILISM

The view that our world is not rooted in a sacred reality, but instead in a partly evil creator or an indifferent process, tends to lead to nihilism—of which there are several types. From a nihilistic perspective, it does not really matter if human civilization is destroyed prematurely by global warming.

One type of nihilism is *existential* nihilism, according to which the world and our lives have no ultimate meaning. For example, a historian discussing the scientific worldview from a neo-Darwinian perspective wrote: "The universe cares nothing for us. Humans are as nothing even in the evolutionary process on earth.... There is no ultimate meaning for humans."[5] If there is no ultimate meaning for humans, why would the premature destruction of human civilization be a tragedy?

There is also *moral* nihilism, according to which we have no moral obligations. John Mackie, who taught philosophy at Oxford, said that, given the truth of atheism, "There are no objective values." For example, "if someone is writhing in agony before your eyes," there is no objective requirement that you should "do something about it if you can."[6] It would follow, therefore, that if you had the power to prevent billions of people from dying for the lack of food and water, there would be no moral obligation to do so.

According to what can be called "climate moral nihilism" in particular, there is no obligation for our generation to replace fossil fuels with clean energy for the sake of future generations. For example, one reader, commenting on a story saying that, if global warming continues, the temperature of the United States will become hellish, responded:

Who cares, I'll probably be dead by then. And if I'm still alive at that point, I still wouldn't care. Giving up big cars, McMansions, and meat for a few degrees of temperature difference is not a tradeoff I or many other people are willing to make.[7]

Finally, a book entitled *The Banalization of Nihilism* discusses "cheerful nihilism," which is "distinguished by an easy-going acceptance of meaninglessness." Cheerful nihilists say, "Let us eat and drink, for tomorrow we die," with "we" meaning humanity as a whole.[8]

One could also speak about another version of cheerful nihilism, in which the motto is, "He who dies with the most toys wins." This would seem to be the motto of some fossil-fuel corporation executives, who continue to deny that fossil-fuel burning causes climate change, even though they know otherwise, and even though they know that fossil fuels are creating a hellish climate for future generations, including their own grandchildren.

Nihilism stands in opposition to what celebrated anthropologist Clifford Geertz called the "religious perspective." Discussing how it prevents moral nihilism, he said that the religious perspective involves sacred symbols, which provide moral motivation. The religious perspective, with its sacred symbols, he explained, supports "the conviction that the values one holds are grounded in the inherent structure of reality, that between the way one ought to live and the way things really are there is an unbreakable inner connection."

Explaining how this conviction accounts for religion's moral vitality, Geertz wrote:

> The powerfully coercive "ought" is felt to grow out of a comprehensive factual "is." ... [The power of sacred symbols] comes from their presumed ability to identify fact with value at the most fundamental level.[9]

Recovering or maintaining a perception of the world as sacred, therefore, will encourage people to want to take care of our common home.

SACREDNESS NOT CONTRADICTED BY EVIL

The problem of evil, which has led to the spread of nihilism, resulted from the fateful decision of early Christian theologians, near the end of the second Christian century, to adopt the doctrine of *creatio ex nihilo*. This doctrine was adopted in favor of the doctrine that God created the world out of chaos, which had been held until then by Christians as well as Jews. This doctrine of *creatio ex nihilo* was later adopted by most Islamic and Jewish theology,[10] so that virtually all theistic traditions have defined God as omnipotent, in the sense that God's will could never be frustrated.

The doctrine of creation out of nothing is completely rejected by process theology, which returns to the old idea of that our universe was created out of chaos. The long-standing problem of evil—how to reconcile the goodness and omnipotence of our creator—is thereby removed. Although Pope Francis did not discuss this issue, I believe (as suggested in Chapter 1) that his view of divine power is similar to that of process theology, which would imply a similar view of the creation.

CREATION OUT OF CHAOS

Whitehead's way of understanding creation out of chaos is based on his view that the world is composed of brief events, which he called "actual occasions." Each occasion involves at least an iota of spontaneity.

In the primordial chaos—meaning the all-pervasive chaos prior to the formation of our universe—these events simply happened at random, rather than having any kind of order. But as our universe began to form, these momentary events—these actual occasions—started forming themselves into enduring individuals.

For example, electronic occasions become organized into electrons, in which each occasion largely repeats its predecessor. This repetition gives the electron stability through time. In the same way, protons and neutrons are enduring individuals consisting of protonic and neutronic occasions. This process continues with the development of increasingly complex individuals, from atoms to macro-molecules, organelles, prokaryotic cells, eukaryotic cells, and the many species of animals, including mammals of various types, with humans being the most complex.

Unlike sticks and stones, animals are not simply aggregational entities, in which the thing as a whole has no overall spontaneity. The behavior of such aggregational entities can be determined by other things, as when the movement of a billiard ball is determined by the movement of another billiard ball or a human hand. By contrast, an animal is self-determining, because it is directed by a very high-level individual, which is composed of very high-level actual occasions, also called "occasions of experience." This very high-level individual is, of course, what we call the mind, psyche, or soul.

The human mind, rather than being simply equatable with the brain—with its approximately 100 billion brain cells (neurons)—is an individual that is far more complex than a neuron (just as a neuron, being an eukaryotic cell, is an individual that is more complex than a prokaryotic cell). The momentary experiences constituting the mind are called "dominant occasions of experience" because, besides integrating all the neuronal experiences into a unified experience, they can also direct the movements of the body as a whole. The human brain is an amazingly complex and sophisticated product of the evolutionary process. But apart from the mind, the brain would be able to achieve little.

FREEDOM AND MORAL EVIL

Although an understandable presentation of creation out of chaos would need to be much more detailed, the essential point here is that all individuals, from the simplest to the most complex, have a degree of spontaneity, with this spontaneity in the higher types of individuals becoming freedom as we humans understand it. Freedom, moreover, is inherent in the creation, so that it cannot be overridden, not even by God. Contrary to traditional free-will theism, God could not occasionally interrupt our freedom to prevent evil. God, therefore, cannot be criticized for not doing so.

Human causation is of two types. On the one hand, there is self-causation (or self-determination), in which a human occasion of experience forms itself. This is freedom. On the other hand, having decided exactly what it was to be, that occasion of experience then exerts influence on subsequent occasions of experience—both those constituting the soul in subsequent moments and those constituting the brain's cells and thereby the cells throughout the body.

Neither type of causation can be controlled by God. For example, in response to the common question of why God did not just convert Hitler away from his murderous plans, the answer is that God could not have done this. God can and does influence all people, but this influence can never be complete control, because all moments of a mind's experience, besides being influenced by events in its brain, necessarily have some power of self-determination. Likewise, when Stalin had decided to kill millions of Soviet citizens, God could not have unilaterally prevented him from giving the orders.

Still another question is often asked: Granted that human beings necessarily have a degree of freedom, why did God create us with such an enormous degree of freedom? Why did God not make human beings with the capacity to enjoy mathematics, music, drama, humor, and human friendship, but without the capacity to invent weapons of mass destruction

The answer is that this would have been impossible. The capacity of humans in civilization to enjoy very high-level types of enjoyment is necessarily the capacity to develop science and technology, through which humans could eventually invent weapons to destroy civilization (assuming, of course, that the planet has the needed physical elements, which is to be discussed below).

NATURAL EVIL

What about the question as to why so many people die horrible deaths from diseases, such as cancer and Alzheimer's disease? Although moral evil can be reconciled with divine goodness by holding that human beings have irrevocable freedom, it is widely assumed that freedom cannot be used to explain the existence of cancer and other diseases. On the basis of process theology, however, that is not the case.

As mentioned above in Chapter 1, actual things have power of their own, so their states and movements cannot be unilaterally determined by God. With regard to actual things that are true individuals, such as ordinary molecules, macromolecules, and bacteria, they have some degree of power to determine themselves, as well as power to influence other things. As discussed in Chapter 4, microbiology has recently shown that bacteria, the lowest forms of life, have the power to make decisions.[11]

Moreover, as discussed in that chapter, the power to make decisions surely did not suddenly come into existence with bacteria. Rather, some lesser degree of spontaneity and decision-making power must exist in the organelles and macromolecules, such as DNA, making up a bacterium. Moreover, given the fact that this power could not have sprung into existence at this level, it must, to some slight degree, go all the way down, as held in process theology's panexperientialism.

From this point of view, evils such as cancer and Alzheimer's disease do not contradict the idea that the creator of our world is perfectly loving. Although God is all-powerful, being the only power that can create a universe, God does not have the power to unilaterally determine the states and movements of things within the created universe. Rather than having been created out of absolute nothingness, our universe embodied a primordial power or activity. Although this power is often called "energy," Whitehead enlarged the notion of energy to that of "creativity," thereby indicating that instantiations of it have the power of self-determination as well as the power to influence others.

Given this perspective, the title of a well-known book about the problem of evil, *Love Almighty and Ills Unlimited*, does not present a mystery. Given the billions of years of evolution since the emergence of living cells, and given the inherent power of cells and their DNA components, it is not surprising, even though God has perfect power and love, that human (and other animal) bodies are afflicted by ills of all types. The same point holds even if we were to limit the evolution to only the past 500 million years since modern types animals appeared. Indeed, it is amazing that humans are generally as healthy as we are.

The blaming of God for cancer and other diseases is rooted in the decision at the end of the second century A.D. to change the description of the origin of our universe from creation out of chaos to *creatio ex nihilo*. Hermogenes, the great but mostly unknown Christian theologian of that time, fought to prevent this disastrous change, because he wanted to ensure the absolute goodness of God as our creator. He is largely unknown today because, having been accused of heresy for denying the brand-new doctrine of *creatio ex nihilo*, his writings were destroyed. We have only a few quotations provided in writings of the time.

Instead of that doctrine, Hermogenes held the then-traditional view that "the ground of the evil present in the world" is "the trace of the original disorder of matter remaining in every created thing." If, by contrast, one supposed God to have created our world out of nothing, "the origin of evil would not be explained," Hermogenes argued, "because as perfect Goodness [God] could only have created good."[12]

What about the question raised by the above-quoted theologian who asked, "Why the Possibility for the Bomb?" His question arose out of his belief that "God certainly could have created the universe and the earth without uranium." That belief would be true only if one accepted the traditional doctrine of omnipotence, according to which God, being able to create anything (except for logical contradictions), could have created our world all at once. With that doctrine, one could do away with the scientific explanation of the Earth, according to which there occurred billions of years of cosmic evolution before our planet was created. With that omnipotence-belief, one could say that the Earth could have been able to support life while not having uranium or any other ingredients from which weapons of mass destruction could have been created.

Process theology, of course, rejects this view. It bases its view of the formation of the Earth on the best scientific evidence and theories available. According to today's science, planets were formed out of the debris from massive explosions of stars called supernovae. These supernovae resulted in various heavy elements, including uranium. Our particular planet evidently resulted from a supernova about 6.5 billion years ago.[13]

There is no good reason to believe that God could have created a planet such as the Earth in any other manner. It seems, therefore, that God could not have created a life-supporting planet devoid of materials through which the planet could be destroyed. By the same token, there is no reason to believe that God could have created a life-supporting planet with no materials that could be used to overheat the planet, making it too hot for the survival of the living creatures that had evolved on it.

CONCLUSION

The overall reconciliation of divine power and worldly evil lies in the necessary tension between value and risk. As discussed in the fourth and fifth chapters, God's aim is to create value. The general aim of evolution is to bring about creatures with the capacity for higher forms of value. But the more highly evolved creatures, being capable of experiencing and sharing higher forms of value, are also necessarily more dangerous.

Human beings provide the fullest illustration. We humans have capacities for value far exceeding those of any other creatures on our planet. But these same capacities necessarily give us the capacities to form armies, use Uranium-235 to make nuclear weapons, and exploit fossil fuels.

The only way for God to avoid human evil on our planet would have been for God not to encourage the emergence of human-like beings. The only way to avoid pain and evil of all types would have been for God not to have created a biocentric universe.

Accordingly, the evils of the world do not contradict the conviction that our planet, along with the universe as a whole, is sacred. We should, therefore, do everything we can to avoid destroying its capacity for life, which makes it especially sacred.

By seeing that nihilism is not justified, and that our world truly is a sacred gift, there can be, in the words of Pope Francis, "the awakening of a new reverence for life" and "the joyful celebration of life" (LS 207). We should also be more able to overcome "our inability to think seriously about future generations" (LS 162).

Thinking seriously about future generations, moreover, requires thinking about the topic of the next chapter, the move to a life-protecting world order.

NOTES

1   St. Augustine, *Enchiridion,* trans. J. F. Shaw, XLI, XLII; in *Basic Writings of St. Augustine,* 2 vols., ed. Whitney J. Oates (New York: Random House, 1948).

2   Jack Cottrell, "The Nature of Divine Sovereignty," in *The Grace of God, the Will of Man,* ed. Clark H. Pinnock (Grand Rapids: Zondervan, 1989), 112.

3   Richard L. Rubenstein, *After Auschwitz: Radical Theology and Contemporary Judaism* (Indianapolis: Bobbs-Merrill, 1966), 46, 64–65, 153.

4   Dale Aukerman, *Darkening Valley: A Biblical Perspective on Nuclear War* (Seabury, 1981), 160–61.

5   William Provine, "Progress in Evolution and Meaning in Life," in Matthew H. Nitecki, ed., *Evolutionary Progress* (Chicago: University of Chicago Press, 1988) 49–74, at 70.

6   John Mackie, *Ethics: Inventing Right and Wrong* (New York: Penguin, 1977), 79–80.

7   Joe Romm, "Our Hellish Future: Definitive NOAA-led Report on U.S. Climate Impacts Warns of Scorching 9 to 111°F Warming Over Most of Inland U.S. by 2090," Climate Progress, 15 June 2009.

8   Karen L. Carr, *The Banalization of Nihilism: Twentieth-Century Responses to Meaninglessness* (Albany, NY: State University of New York Press, 1992).

9   Clifford Geertz, *Islam Observed: Religious Development in Morocco and Indonesia* (New Haven: Yale University Press, 1968), 97; Geertz, *Interpretation of Cultures: Selected Essays* (New York: Basic Books, 1973), 126–27.

10   Austin Farrer, *Love Almighty and Ills Unlimited: An Essay on Providence and Evil* (Fontana, 1962).

11   See, for example, Matthew Russell, "How Do Bacteria Make Decisions?" Frontiers, 23 January 2014. For more on this, see the section, Decision-Making Bacteria, in Chapter 4, "Consciousness," in David Ray Griffin, *God Exists but Gawd Does Not* (Anoka, MN: Process Century Press, 2016).

12   Gerhard May, *Creatio Ex Nihilo: The Doctrine of "Creation out of Nothing" in Early Christian Thought,* trans. A. S. Worrall (Edinburgh: T. & T. Clark, 1994), 141–42.

13   "The Cosmic Origins of Uranium," World Nuclear Association, November 2006.

CHAPTER SEVEN

Life-Protecting World Order

Although many people agree with Pope Francis and process theologians that it is life, not the economy, that is sacred, this conviction will remain largely ineffective unless there is a life-protecting world order, in which this idea will be fundamental to the practices of individuals, communities, businesses, economies, technologies, and governments at every level. The encyclical of Pope Francis culminates in a call for such a world order.

The world order, he says, should be based on a fundamental principle of Catholic social teaching, namely:

> [T]he principle of subsidiarity, which grants freedom to develop the capabilities present at every level of society, while also demanding a greater sense of responsibility for the common good from those who wield greater power. (LS 196)

With regard to the climate, the nation-states have the most political power to deal with it. But that power is inadequate, for reasons to be discussed below.

Having said, "It cannot be emphasized enough how everything is interconnected" (LS 138), the pope added: "Interdependence obliges us to think of one world with a common plan" (LS 164). A common plan

97

is necessary, he explained, because the problems "cannot be resolved by unilateral actions on the part of individual countries" (LS 164).

Referring to the most obvious reason why a common plan is necessary, "the use of highly polluting fossil fuels," said the pope, "needs to be progressively replaced without delay" (LS 165). But also, he pointed out, there needs to be planning for a "sustainable and diversified agriculture," a better "management of marine and forest resources," and "ensuring universal access to drinking water" (LS 164). More generally, said Pope Francis, the world needs "an agreement on systems of governance for the whole range of so-called 'global commons'" (LS 174). In particular, while reducing pollution, the world needs a plan for the "development of poorer countries and regions" (LS 175).

To develop a common plan, the pope holds, we need international institutions. Such institutions are necessary not only because unilateral decisions by the various nations of the world would not result in a common approach, but also because even the nation-states have been weakened. Economic and financial sectors, having become transnational, tend to "prevail over the political." Accordingly,

> [I]t is essential to devise stronger and more efficiently organized international institutions, with functionaries who are appointed fairly by agreement among national governments, and empowered to impose sanctions. (LS 175)

Making his point even clearer, the pope said: "Global regulatory norms are needed to impose obligations and prevent unacceptable actions" (LS 173).

In believing that without such norms, civilization will simply continue to drift towards disaster, the pope is reflecting the point made above in Chapter 1, namely, that calling God the "all-powerful creator" does not mean that we could count on God to rescue us from our foolish fossil-fuel ways.

PROCESS THINKERS ON GLOBAL ORDER

John Cobb and I published an article some years ago that expressed agreement with "the Catholic principle of subsidiarity, which stipulates that decisions should be made as close to the local level as possible." We added, however, that there are some issues that must be regulated at the national level and still others, such as pollution, that "can only be effectively regulated at the global level." We pointed out, however, that the global human community "has no means by which it can exercise self-determination."[1]

With regard to the economy, we said, it should be subjected to political control (rather than having politics controlled by economic interests). Although there are strong reasons to oppose a global government, we concluded,

> Our economy is in fact global. For this reason, it cannot be controlled by nations or even by regional bodies. Unless the economy is radically changed, only a strong centralized, global government can regulate it for the common good.[2]

In *For the Common Good*, Cobb along with Herman Daly addressed the issue of global governance. Pointing out the need for transnational institutions through which communities of nations can express their common interests, they considered it good that nation-states have had to modify their claims to absolute sovereignty. Some of this commonality is expressed in the World Court and the United Nations. However, they added, current trends "are leading to the wrong kind of centralization."

Here they were speaking primarily of the North American Free Trade Agreement (NAFTA) and the General Agreement on Tariffs and Trade (GATT), which vests much authority in the Multilateral Trade Organization (MTO). In the name of reducing barriers to trade, it has been given the authority to "overrule the laws of the United States government and of individuals states, such as those safeguarding the environment." Calling this unacceptable, they declared: "Any group with that kind of power must be responsible to the people and not to economic interests alone. That means that it must have the character of a government."[3]

While saying they do not favor that degree of centralization of power, they added:

> If the world moves further toward an integrated global economy, thereby requiring centralization of power for the adjudication of disputes, then this power should be vested in a political body.... If this body had powers comparable to those to be invested in MTO, this would move the United Nations a long way toward becoming a world government. We consider centralization of power under the United Nations far preferable to the concentration of power in a group that is not responsive to political influence and whose function is purely economic.

Contrasting this idea with a full-scale global government, they added, a global political body should not have power over every dimension of life and society. A "global organization should have power only over global matters."[4]

More recently, the proposed Trans-Pacific Partnership (TPP) involving 12 nations, which would cover over 40 percent of the global GNP, was almost universally denounced by environmental groups. The TPP, they warned, "could have catastrophic repercussions for climate change, including giving corporations the power to sue governments that try to limit polluting industries."[5]

Regardless of the ultimate fate of the proposed TPP, the attempt to authorize it suggests that the business world will continue to try to undermine climate regulations whenever such rules are viewed as limiting profits. The creation of a global agency is needed to prevent, in the pope's words, the "absolute autonomy of the marketplace" resulting in a "new tyranny," which "relentlessly imposes its own laws and rules" (EG 56).

SUMMARY

Process thinkers agree with the pope's call for a global political framework that can protect our common, sacred home from the incessant drive to maximize corporate profits, regardless of their damage to our climate and hence human beings, present and future. Only some type of global government would have the power to prevent the idolatry of money from turning our planet into a hell.

NOTES

1   John B. Cobb, Jr. and David Ray Griffin, "A Process Alternative to Pax Americana," Center for Process Studies.

2   Ibid.

3   Herman E. Daly and John B. Cobb, Jr., *For the Common Good: Redirecting the Economy toward Community, the Environment, and a Sustainable Future,* updated and expanded edition (Boston: Beacon Press, 1994), 353.

4   Ibid.

5   Samantha Page, "The TPP Could Have Disastrous Results for the Climate, Environmental Groups Warn," Climate Progress, 15 May 2015.

CHAPTER EIGHT

Conclusion

THE PURPOSE OF THIS BOOK is to show that the position of Whitehead-based process thought on climate change and related matters is remarkably similar to that of the 2015 encyclical of Pope Francis. This similarity is important for two reasons.

First, in light of the fact that process thought and the pope's encyclical, embodying a new expression of Catholic social thought, come out of very different traditions, the similarity allows each to add credibility to the other. Second, process thought, embodying a long-standing type of philosophical theology that is consistent with today's best science and has been growing in influence, can be used to support dimensions of the pope's encyclical that might seem incredible to modern minds.

As the previous chapters have shown, the pope's encyclical and process thought agree on at least eight major points.

INTRINSIC VALUE IN THE ENTIRE WORLD

Both the pope and process thought are strongly against anthropocentrism, according to which the only value of non-human nature is the value it has for human beings. Both the pope and process thinkers regard all levels of nature as having intrinsic value. This is one basis for considering the entire world sacred.

GOD IN THE WORLD, THE WORLD IN GOD

Rather than imagining the world to be an external product of its creator, both process thought and the pope's encyclical portray God and the world as intimately related. Exemplifying the two-fold relation that process thinkers call "panentheism," God is said to be internal to the creatures while those creatures internal to God. By virtue of this double relationship, the world is even more strongly portrayed as sacred.

THE UNIVERSE CREATED BY GOD

The pope and process theologians both portray the universe as the creation of God. The dominant forms of modern science and philosophy have, to be sure, tried to explain everything—from the formation of the universe to the evolutionary emergence of human beings—without reference to any kind of purposive creator. Process thinkers, however, have explained why a divine creator is needed, both for the upward trend of the evolutionary process and for the fine-tuning of the universe, which allowed for the emergence of life. God is also seen as necessary to provide a home for the logical, mathematical, and other forms required for distinctive human capacities. The whole evolutionary process, therefore, should be considered sacred.

SACREDNESS NOT UNDERMINED BY EVIL

While some atheists deny the need for a fine-tuner by appealing to the multiverse hypothesis, others agree that the fine-tuning implies a creator, but argue that the problem of evil shows that the creator is less than perfectly good. From this perspective, the universe could not be considered sacred. However, process thought explains that the existence of evil in the world—both moral and natural—does not contradict the creator's perfect goodness. Although God is all-powerful, in the sense of being the only being that could create a universe, this does not imply that God can prevent evil, because finite entities necessarily have their own power, which cannot be overridden. That the pope would support this view is suggested by various statements by him — such as his declaration that the world was created from "love," which is the "fundamental moving force in all created things," rather than from "arbitrary omnipotence," and his rejection of the idea that God is "a magician, with a magic wand able to do everything." Seen in this light, the evils of the world do not contradict its sacredness.

SERIOUSNESS OF THE CLIMATE CRISIS

With such a view of God, it is no surprise that the pope does not agree with those people who say that, given divine omnipotence, we do not need to worry about climate change. Opposing climate complacency, both the pope and process thinkers argue that the world must end its use of fossil fuels quickly, before it destroys the supreme products on our planet of the evolutionary process, which it took God many billions of years to produce.

ETHICS OF THE COMMON GOOD VS. RELATIVISM

Process thinkers and the pope's encyclical both reject relativism, according to which there are no indisputable facts and principles to guide our lives. Besides saying that moral principles are capable of being either true or false, they also share the truth of the principle that our social policies should be centered around the idea of the common good. They also emphasize that the common good includes that of future generations, so that we need to protect a livable climate indefinitely. They also agree, finally, that the concern for the common good means that climate policies need to be aimed simultaneously at saving the climate and saving the poor, who will increasingly suffer disproportionately from climate change.

ECONOMIC IDOLATRY

Speaking of "economism" and "growth idolatry," process thinkers agree completely with the pope's denunciation of "the idolatry of money" and the "deified market." The idea that the market best promotes the common good is one of the big lies of the age, because accepting the rule by the market destroys the environment as well as increases the gap between the rich and the poor. Another big lie is that unending growth is possible. In stating that more economic growth is not progress when it leads to a decrease in the quality of life, the pope is supported by Herman Daly's argument that the increase of the GDP of rich nations is really *uneconomic* growth. The devotion to the growth of money, process thinkers agree with Pope Francis, is idolatry, because it has replaced devotion to God and thereby the good of the whole. Instead, there needs to be "degrowth," followed by a steady-state economy.

NEED FOR A GLOBAL POLITICAL BODY

Both process thinkers and the pope say that the above agreement—that life rather than money is sacred—will remain impotent without the creation of a life-protecting global order. Specifically, they say that, in line with the principle of subsidiarity, there needs to be an international political body or agency to deal with issues that can be regulated only at the global level, such as the global economy and the global ecological crisis. Otherwise, there is no way to prevent market idolatry from further increasing poverty and destroying civilization.

****

This book has been written with the hope that it will help increase the effectiveness of the encyclical letter of Pope Francis, *Laudato Si': On the Care for Our Common Home.*

INDEX